The SEASON *of* REBUILDING

PATRICK M. MORLEY

LIFE**WAY** PRESS
Nashville, Tennessee

Dedication

To Tommy Boroughs, Chuck Green, Chuck Mitchell, and Ken Moar—
Thanks for helping me find God's grace
in each of my seasons.

7200-93
ISBN 0-8054-9786-2
Dewey Decimal Classification: 248.842
Subject Heading: MEN \ RELIGIOUS LIFE
This book is the text for course CG-0181 in the subject
area Personal Life in the Christian Growth Study Plan
Printed in the United States of America

Acknowledgements
The Curriculum Products are based on
The Seven Seasons of a Man's Life, by Patrick Morley, and
created under license granted by Thomas Nelson, Inc.
Unless otherwise indicated, Scripture quotations are from
the Holy Bible, *New International Version,*
copyright © 1973,1978,1984, by International Bible Society
Scripture quotations marked NKJV are from
the *New King James Version.* Copyright © 1979, 1980, 1982,
Thomas Nelson, Inc., Publishers.
Scripture quotations marked TLB are taken from *The Living
Bible.* Copyright © Tyndale House Publishers, Wheaton,
Illinois, 1971. Used by permission.

Design: Edward Crawford
Cover Illustration: Michael Schwab
Icons: © CSA Archive
Curriculum Writer: Larry Keefauver
Coordinating Editor: David Delk

LifeWay Press
127 Ninth Avenue, North
Nashville, Tennessee 37234

CONTENTS

THE SEASON OF REBUILDING

INTRODUCTION

WELCOME to *The Season of Rebuilding*. The Season of Rebuilding is exactly what it implies. Something was built. It didn't turn out exactly as planned. And now it is time to reevaluate and rebuild. I want you to know...

You are not alone. I have discovered that every man experiences seven seasons during his life.

 The Season of Reflection

 The Season of Building

 The Season of Crisis

 The Season of Renewal

 The Season of Rebuilding

 The Season of Suffering

 The Season of Success

I have prepared four books in this collection to help you explore these seasons. This book focuses on the season of rebuilding.

Each week during the next six weeks you will have five daily studies to read and complete. You will need 20 to 30 minutes each day.

Each day a BIG IDEA will be presented. The BIG IDEA (identified with this symbol ◆) captures the main point for that day's lesson in one sentence. The rest of the material for that day amplifies, expands, explains, and applies the BIG IDEA.

You will also read other statements with which you will highly identify. Let me encourage you to underline, make notes, and write down questions about ideas you don't agree with or understand. If you are studying with a group, bring up your questions with the other men.

For added review, a list of key ideas called *The Bottom Line* appears at the end of each day's lesson.

Let me urge you to find a group of men to study with you. Use the Leader Guide on pages 128-141. This investment will bring a great return.

You and your spiritual pilgrimage are the focal point of this study. The subject is God and wisdom to live under His authority and grace. So, in each lesson you will be encouraged to apply the truths and principles to your life situation.

I pray that God will use this study in a wonderful and powerful way in your life. Millions of men are experiencing a hunger for God. They want to think more deeply about their lives. They are seeking to become the spiritual leaders of their homes and discover God's will for their lives. Whichever season of life you find yourself in, this study will encourage you to keep going.

Would you like to learn more about the ministry of Patrick Morley? Partnering with churches and ministries, our vision is to reach every man in America with compelling opportunities to be transformed by Jesus Christ. Our strategies include:
- Man in the Mirror Seminars
- The Man in the Mirror Leadership Institute
- Publishing Christian literature
- Serving churches and other ministries
- TGIF Men's Ministry in Orlando, Florida

If you would like to receive 3 sample issues of our monthly newsletter for men, send your name and address to:

Patrick Morley Ministries
198 Wilshire Blvd.
Casselberry, FL 32707

LIFE'S SEASONS

There is a time for everything,
and a season for every activity
  under heaven:
a time to be born and a time to die,
a time to plant and a time to uproot,
a time to kill and a time to heal,
a time to tear down and a time to build,
a time to weep and a time to laugh,
a time to mourn and a time to dance,
a time to scatter stones and a time to
  gather them,
a time to embrace and a time to refrain,
a time to search and a time to give up,
a time to keep and a time to throw away,
a time to tear and a time to mend,
a time to be silent and a time to speak,
a time to love and a time to hate,
a time for war and a time for peace.

—Ecclesiastes 3:1-8

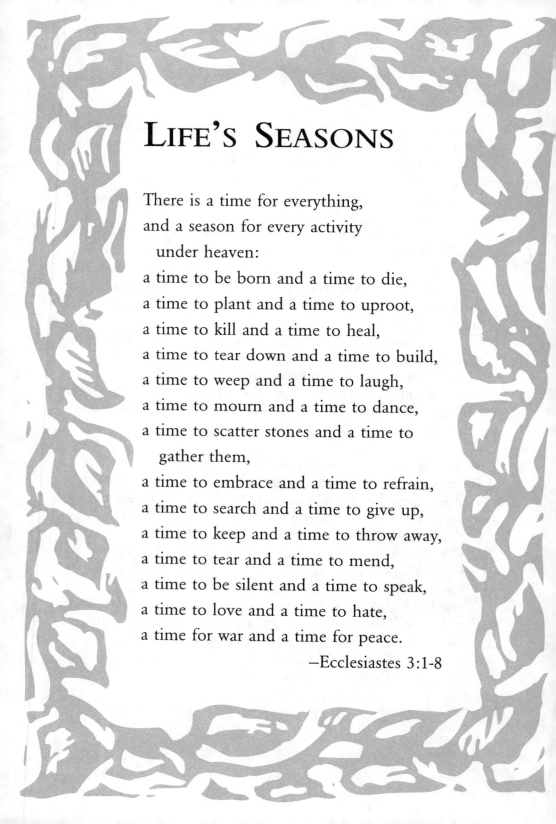

The Season of Rebuilding

FOUR CRUCIAL CONVERSIONS

It was a long, hot summer. I was in the midst of the third major phase of my spiritual pilgrimage—the commitment to the God who is. At the beginning of the summer I was walking closely with my Lord. Still, I had no idea how powerfully my flesh had deceived me. What follows are some lessons I've learned at a deeper level.

In 1991, I responded to a new calling in my life to move from real estate to ministry. Although I still have business interests, I have no day-to-day operating responsibilities.

For the next couple of years I worked extremely hard to become established in my new calling. One day I was standing around talking to one of our men's ministry leaders, and he made a statement that startled me. He said, "Pat, don't try to make up for lost time." *Zap!*

Suddenly, I realized I was working hard because I felt I should be producing at a certain level due to my age and experience. It was as though I assumed God made a mistake by having me in business 20 years, so I was going to help Him get me where I needed to be by working extra hard.

Since that day, I have pondered my friend's statement over and over again. God doesn't make mistakes. All the years you and I have spent and invested to this point, whether wisely or not, can be used by God to shape our lives. There is no such thing as a wasted past. The past is one of the ingredients God uses to produce the character of Christ in us. When God calls us in a new direction, He will equip us to accomplish everything He intends without our having to "make up for lost time."

We will explore four crucial conversions in the Season of Rebuilding. The term *conversion* is most often used to identify the experience of becoming a Christian. In this context, conversion will be used to identify the transformation that occurs after the initial salvation experience. Another term used is *sanctification*. Transformation or sanctification is conversion from the old life of the flesh to the new life in the Spirit that takes place over an entire lifetime.

At the root of being transformed is your desire to become Christlike. As you examine your life, you will uncover the areas where you need to purge selfish desires and allow God's Spirit to rebuild your motives **(heart)**, your mind **(head)**, your use of time **(calendar)**, and your possessions **(wallet)**. During this first week, you will evaluate:

- The motives for the good deeds you do in life.
- How to face the difficult challenge of moving from "the flesh" to a new life "in the Spirit."
- Giving your heart to Jesus Christ.
- Whether you are still clinging to a secular worldview or have truly accepted a Christian worldview.
- If Jesus has control over your time and your possessions.

In your examination of these four crucial areas, I invite you to spend time in prayer, Bible study, reflection, and self-evaluation. Allow God's Spirit to speak to you about the areas of your life that need rebuilding through His power and grace.

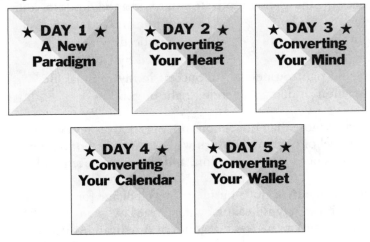

| ★ DAY 1 ★ A New Paradigm | ★ DAY 2 ★ Converting Your Heart | ★ DAY 3 ★ Converting Your Mind |
| ★ DAY 4 ★ Converting Your Calendar | ★ DAY 5 ★ Converting Your Wallet | |

Memorize and meditate on this Scripture passage every day:

Therefore, if anyone is in Christ, he is a new creation; the old has gone, the new has come! (2 Corinthians 5:17).

A NEW PARADIGM

A newly committed or recommitted man ought to rethink everything he has been taught about what Christianity is. I have rediscovered this frequently in my Christian walk. The Bible says the flesh, our indwelling sin, is deceitful. The Bible says the flesh is wicked. The Bible says the flesh is weak. However, the flesh is most deceitful, most wicked, and most weak when disguised as piety.

◆

The only thing worse than flesh is pious flesh.

Pious flesh often is the result of subscribing to a cultural form of Christianity rather than a biblical form of Christianity.

Check the things that motivate you to do good deeds in your life.
- ❏ Pride
- ❏ Joy in serving Jesus
- ❏ Praise of others
- ❏ Piety and righteousness
- ❏ Desire to earn God's approval
- ❏ Being noticed by others
- ❏ Being used by God
- ❏ Success in my spiritual life
- ❏ Satisfaction of doing something right or good

Perhaps even more than our actions do, our motives reveal the paradigm, the model or pattern, by which we live. And the bottom line is that many of us need a paradigm shift, and some of us need a whole new paradigm.

Biblical Christianity is not a business. It is medicine for people sick unto death. Christianity is healing by the Great Physician. Too often we want people to think in narrow categories of American, Aristotelian, linear logic—we want to chart Jesus on a graph. We can't do that. God won't let us.

You see, Biblical Christianity—being an instrument of God, working in and for His kingdom—is a radically different model from what we are accustomed to in our culture. Trusting Jesus Christ not only saves us, but it is supposed to change us as well. *Salvation* takes place in an instant of fully yielding the control of our lives to the saving grace of our Lord Jesus Christ. *Sanctification,* however, is the lifelong process of each day becoming more like Jesus. We don't change ourselves; we are changed by the power of His Spirit at work in us.

Read the following Scriptures. Underline ways we are changed by God's Spirit.

And we, who with unveiled faces all reflect the Lord's glory, are being transformed into his likeness with ever-increasing glory, which comes from the Lord, who is the Spirit (2 Corinthians 3:18).

For Christ's love compels us, because we are convinced that one died for all, and therefore all died. And he died for all, that those who live should no longer live for themselves but for him who died for them and was raised again.

So from now on we regard no one from a worldly point of view. Though we once regarded Christ in this way, we do so no longer. Therefore, if anyone is in Christ, he is a new creation; the old has gone, the new has come! All this is from God, who reconciled us to himself through Christ and gave us the ministry of reconciliation (2 Corinthians 5:14-18).

Therefore, I urge you, brothers, in view of God's mercy, to offer your bodies as living sacrifices, holy and pleasing to God—this is your spiritual act of worship. Do not conform any longer to the pattern of this world, but be transformed by the renewing of your mind. Then you will be able to test and approve what God's will is—his good, pleasing and perfect will (Romans 12:1-2).

Look at all the verbs in these passages that relate to being a new creation in Jesus Christ. Circle the ones that are working most powerfully in your life right now.

Let's look at some of the ingredients of being Biblical Christians.

❑ We are compelled by Christ's love.

❑ We no longer live for ourselves but for Him.

❑ We have a whole new way of looking at people.

❑ We are new creations in Jesus.

❑ The old nature is gone; a new nature has come.

❑ We are reconciled to God.

❑ We have been entrusted with a ministry of reconciling others to God in Christ.

Put a check by the ingredient God is working on in your life right now. Circle the ingredient that needs more work by His Spirit.

Many times we are shaped more by our culture than by Christ. This is especially true in four crucial areas of life. Sanctification means that our *hearts*, *minds*, *calendars*, and *wallets* will be changed, converted, and made new in Jesus Christ.

Jesus calls men to a radically different way of thinking and living. It is an altogether different paradigm from what many of us have been led to believe. This change is nothing to fear. In exchange for all the worldly, fleshly desires, we will be filled with the fruit of the Spirit. We will become like Jesus, transformed into His image.

Review today's lesson. What was the most meaningful statement or Scripture you read?

_____

_____

Reword the statement or Scripture into a prayer response to God.

_____

_____

What does God want you to do in response to today's study?

_____

_____

Review your Scripture memory verse for the week–2 Corinthians 5:17– and write it below.

_____

_____

The Bottom Line
- The only thing worse than flesh is pious flesh.
- Trusting Jesus Christ not only saves us, but it is supposed to change us as well.
- Sanctification means that our *hearts, minds, calendars,* and *wallets* will be changed, converted, and made new in Jesus Christ.

CONVERTING YOUR HEART

The most difficult challenge of Christian living is the conversion from the old life of the flesh to the new life in the Spirit. In fact, we relapse, but we can be encouraged that it occurs less frequently the longer and closer we walk with Jesus. So the challenge is to walk increasingly in the Spirit, not in the flesh.

Bishop William Temple said, "Conversion is to give as much of your self as you can to as much of God as you can understand, and to do so every day." *Conversion* means "to transform, to change from one use to another."

Conversion from the old life of the flesh to the new life in the Spirit necessarily takes place over an entire lifetime. We are not called upon to wear size 10 shoes when we have grown only to size 4 feet. The more we know, the better the quality of life with Christ.

A man in the rebuilding season of life must yield areas to the sufficiency of Christ. This yielding is a growing commitment. Four areas in particular that need to be converted to the ways of the Spirit of Jesus deserve special attention: the **heart,** the **head,** the **calendar,** and the **wallet.** Today we will explore converting our hearts.

Your heart is at the center of your spiritual life. The Bible teaches us the importance of the heart.

Read each of the following Scriptures and jot down what they say about the heart.

Text	Your Heart is...
Above all else, guard your heart, for it is the wellspring of life (Proverbs 4:23).	_____ _____
I will give you a new heart and put a new spirit in you; I will remove your heart of stone and give you a heart of flesh (Ezekiel 36:26).	_____ _____ _____ _____

For it is with your heart that you
believe and are justified, and it is
with your mouth that you confess
and are saved (Romans 10:9-10).

    _____

    _____

    _____

    _____

My heart is steadfast, O God, my heart
is steadfast (Psalm 57:7).

    _____

    _____

Perhaps the greatest risk of walking with Jesus is that we might lose our first love. What starts out as a wonderful love relationship is reduced to an endless repetition of religious tasks and activities—all intended to please Him.

◆

**What Christ wants most is not what we can do for Him.
He wants us.**

Christ wants a relationship. Christ wants us to talk with Him and spend time with Him the same way we do with our wives or best friends. It is not enough to give Jesus your life. You must also give Him your heart.

Is there any emotion in your relationship with Jesus Christ? Is He your first love? In John 15:13-15, Jesus calls us His friends: "You are my friends if you do what I command you. I no longer call you servants, because a servant does not know his master's business. Instead, I have called you friends, for everything that I learned from my Father I have made known to you."

Below, list the qualities you expect from a best friend.
A best friend...

❑ _____   ❑ _____   ❑ _____

❑ _____   ❑ _____   ❑ _____

Check those qualities you have in your relationship with Jesus. What's missing? What can you do to make Jesus even more of a best friend?

15

If we love God with all our hearts, then we will serve Him with all our might. We serve God because we love Him. In other words, serving God with the totality of our strength and being will not bring us to love Jesus. Rather, out of our overflow of loving Jesus, His love compels us to do something wonderful for Him because of the rich deposits of gratitude building up in our hearts.

How is your heart toward Jesus? Mark an x where your relationship is right now with Christ.

Hot	Lukewarm	Growing Cold

Know Him	Learning of Him	Know about Him

Intimate friendship	Acquaintance	Distant from Him

Heart of flesh	Heart of stone
soft toward Jesus	hardened toward Him

If you need a new or renewed heart for Jesus, pray right now and surrender totally to Him; and ask God to give you a new heart for Him. Write that prayer below. If your heart is intimate with Jesus, thank Him for the new heart He has given you.

_____

_____

_____

_____

_____

_____

Review today's lesson. What was the most meaningful statement or Scripture you read?

_____

_____

What does God want you to do in response to today's study?

_____

_____

The Bottom Line
- Conversion from the old life of the flesh to the new life in the Spirit necessarily takes place over an entire lifetime.
- Perhaps the greatest risk of walking with Jesus is that we would lose our first love.
- What Christ wants most is not what we can do for Him. He wants us.
- If we love God with all our hearts, then we will serve Him with all our might.

CONVERTING YOUR MIND

Yesterday we considered Christ's call for us to surrender our hearts to Him. But caution is necessary. Devotion to God is paramount, but this alone may lead one to become what we could call an "emotional hearer." Devotion must be accompanied by knowledge of God's Word. Today we will consider the mind.

Biblical Christianity is a thinking man's religion; it is a religion of the mind. It consists of specific truths, and these truths are knowable. We make choices based upon what we know. It is, therefore, crucial to know what we believe and why. It is essential to the work of God's kingdom to think and decide rightly.

◆

**It is not enough to give Jesus your heart.
You must also give Him your head.**

How do we give our heads to Jesus? By developing a Christian worldview. How would you define the term *worldview*?

_____

_____

Dr. Ron Nash defines worldview as "a collection of answers to the most important questions in life."[1] By definition, a worldview is a religious choice because the most important questions in life consider, among other things, the meaning of life, and the existence and nature of God.

Critical to this is what you choose to put into your mind or what you allow your mind to dwell upon in your thought life. Paul writes in 2 Corinthians that we must pull down arguments and pretensions in our minds while we take every thought captive for Jesus Christ.

18

For though we live in the world, we do not wage war as the world does. The weapons we fight with are not the weapons of the world. On the contrary, they have divine power to demolish strongholds. We demolish arguments and every pretension that sets itself up against the knowledge of God, and we take captive every thought to make it obedient to Christ (2 Corinthians 10:3-5).

Paul wrote earlier in 1 Corinthians that we have the mind of Christ. "For who has known the mind of the Lord that he may instruct him?" But we have the mind of Christ (1 Corinthians 2:16).

Check the three things that most influence your daily thoughts.
- ❏ Reading Scripture
- ❏ Listening to my critics
- ❏ Watching television
- ❏ Listening to music
- ❏ Listening to my wife
- ❏ The ideas of unbelievers around me
- ❏ Praying and talking with God
- ❏ Reading the newspaper
- ❏ Reading Christian books
- ❏ Listening to Christian teaching

Perhaps you would like to join me in saying, *"Lord, I confess my culture. Relieve me of the burden of my culture. Help me to think biblically. Help me develop a Christian worldview. Let me see Jesus. Amen."*

Talk with your pastor or an employee of a Christian book store and ask what books you might read to begin inputting into your thought life concepts from a biblical worldview. Spend time in a Christian Bible study listening to God's Word discussed. Develop a quiet time each day in prayer, reading and studying God's Word.

"Apply your heart to instruction and your ears to words of knowledge" (Proverbs 23:12). Pray the Lord will give you the power to take every thought captive. Dwell in your mind and heart on His Word. Speak the following verse out loud:

"And the peace of God,...will guard [my] heart and [my] mind in Christ Jesus!" (Philippians 4:7).

Review today's lesson. What was the most meaningful statement or Scripture you read?

_____

_____

What does God want you to do in response to today's study?

_____

_____

Review this week's memory verse by saying it out loud three times. Reflect on it as you go about the remainder of your day.

The Bottom Line
- Devotion must be accompanied by knowledge of God's Word.
- It is not enough to give Jesus your heart; you must also give Him your head.

---

[1]Ronald Nash, *Faith and Reason* (Grand Rapids: Academie Books, 1988), 21ff.

CONVERTING YOUR CALENDAR

One day I was invited to have lunch with a wealthy, retired Christian businessman. During the course of lunch, I asked him, "What do you do with your time?"

"I do whatever I want to do," he replied a bit too quickly. I remember thinking at the time that he probably had not thought deeply about the responsibilities of Christian wealth.

What was he really saying? He was making a statement about how he runs his life—about how he had dealt with the issue, "Who's in charge?"

◆

**It's not enough to give Jesus your heart and your head.
You must also give Him control over your time.**

All of us start each day with the same size "time account." We all get the same number of hours, minutes, and seconds. And at the end of the day we will have withdrawn and spent them all. But how and where we've spent this precious commodity says a lot about who is in charge of our lives. So, who determines how you use your time?

Prioritize the persons or things that demand the most of your time by ordering the following list from 1—demands the least amount of my time, to 10—demands the most amount of my time.

_____ Myself

_____ Wife

_____ Family

_____ Friends

_____ Church

_____ Jesus

_____ Hobbies and/or sports (participating or viewing)

_____ Job

_____ Television

_____ Ministry to others

Calculate how you spend your time. Beside the following activities, write the approximate percentage of time you spend each week in that activity.

	Percentage of Time Used
Worship	_____
Prayer and Bible study	_____
Wife and Family	_____
Watching television, listening to the radio	_____
Working at home and on the job	_____
Leisure time, recreation	_____
Serving and ministering to others	_____
Sleep	_____

In describing his relationship with Christ, author Gary Smalley paints this picture of how he spends his time. Each day when he awakens, he takes his empty cup, gets in line, and goes to meet with Jesus. Then during the day, he empties out his cup serving others. The next day, he gets up, takes his empty cup, once again stands in line, and starts all over again.

Jesus says, "And if anyone gives even a cup of cold water to one of these little ones because he is my disciple, I tell you the truth, he will certainly not lose his reward" (Matthew 10:42). Are you living your life selfishly or serving others in Jesus' name? Jesus says, "I tell you the truth, whatever you did for one of the least of these brothers of mine, you did it for me" (Matthew 25:40).

The Bible teaches us to use our time wisely. Here are some biblical texts that reveal God's intentions for our use of time. Read each passage and circle the one that speaks most directly to you about your use of time for Him.

"Whoever obeys his command will come to no harm,
　　and the wise heart will know the proper time and procedure.
For there is a proper time and procedure for every matter,
　　though a man's misery weighs heavily upon him"
　　　　　　　　　　　　　　　　(Ecclesiastes 8:5-6).

"Let us not become weary in doing good, for at the proper time we will reap a harvest if we do not give up. Therefore, as we have opportunity, let us do good to all people, especially to those who belong to the family of believers" (Galatians 6:9-10).

"Be very careful, then, how you live—not as unwise but as wise, making the most of every opportunity, because the days are evil" (Ephesians 5:15-16).

How do you determine the use of your time? Mark an x on the bar to indicate where you are right now.

I let the Lord guide me.   I do whatever I want to do.

If Jesus stood in front of you, what might He say to you about the use of your time? Would Jesus confront you about wasting precious time in life? Would He challenge you to spend more of your time witnessing and serving in the kingdom of God? Imagine facing Jesus right now. Briefly write what you believe He would say to you about your use of time.

_____

_____

How do you give your calendar to Jesus? If your heart and your mind have truly been converted, your calendar will follow. You convert your calendar by telling Jesus, "I will go anywhere You want me to go, do anything You want me to do, and be anything You want me to be." This is the decision to convert your time to Christ. Why not tell this to Jesus right now?

Review today's lesson. What was the most meaningful statement or Scripture you read?

_____

_____

23

Reword the statement or Scripture into a prayer response to God.

_____

_____

What does God want you to do in response to today's study?

_____

_____

The Bottom Line
- It's not enough to give Jesus your heart and your head. You must also give Him control over your time.
- You convert your calendar by telling Jesus, "I will go anywhere You want me to go, do anything You want me to do, and be anything You want me to be."

CONVERTING YOUR WALLET

Most of my early life was devoted to thinking about the next thing I wanted to acquire. That's because I was a materialist. Materialism is buying things you don't need with money you don't have to impress people you don't like!

I would like you to reflect carefully on what I am about to say: Our Christian culture tends to teach that we own our money and should give some of it back to God. That is not what the Bible teaches.

◆

God owns everything and calls us to be stewards of 100 percent of our money.

A steward is a manager. God allows us to manage and control some of His financial resources during our lives. It is our responsibility to manage these in a way that is in line with God's purpose and goals for our lives.

As stewards, we should be wise in the way we acquire and use money. God calls us to earn money diligently, invest money wisely, give money generously, save money frugally, and spend money thoughtfully.

How are you doing in your stewardship of the resources that God has given you to manage? Check any of the following areas that are a part of your current lifestyle, and circle all the areas where you need more work.

- ❏ Working hard to earn money
- ❏ Investing money for the future
- ❏ Giving generously (10% or more)
- ❏ Saving for retirement
- ❏ Saving for children's college
- ❏ Spending money thoughtfully
- ❏ Having adequate insurance to protect assets and family

Biblical Christians will have a new orientation to money. One way to evaluate if your heart has been truly converted is to answer the question, "Has your wallet been converted too?"

Evaluate your use of the resources God has given you by placing an x on the following line to indicate where you see yourself.

I use money however I want.   I view myself as God's steward.

Many Christians assume they are directly giving a higher percentage of their income to God's work than they really are. While opinions vary, I think you should calculate your giving by including all sources of income minus only business expenses (if you have them).

What percentage of your income do you believe you are investing in churches and ministries at this time?
❑ Under 1%   ❑ 1-4%   ❑ 5-9%   ❑ 10-15%   ❑ Over 15%

Look at your last tax return or do a quick calculation from your checkbook to determine what percentage you have really given over the last 12 months. Is it the same as your estimate above?

"Being a steward is an attitude, a way of looking at life as a caretaker. It is an approach to our faith—it's looking out not only for our own interests but also for the interests of others."[1]

What will happen if we yield control of our money to Jesus? Matthew 6:21 says, to paraphrase, "Where your wallet is there will your heart be also." If we give our money to Jesus, He will draw us closer still into the safety of His pasture. He will release us from our bondage to money. He will set us free to serve Him financially with gladness.

It is not enough to give Jesus your heart, your head, and your calendar. You must also give Him control over your money. Have you ever said to Christ, "I not only give you control of my heart, but I give you control of my finances"? If not, perhaps there will be no better time than this moment.

You may want to express your desire to convert areas of your life to God in prayer. Use your own words or pray the prayer on the following page.

Lord, I want to be sold out to Jesus. I will go wherever You want me to go, do whatever You want me to do, and be whatever You want me to be. I want to be out-and-out for Christ. I want to be committed to the gospel of the kingdom. I want to be converted in my heart, my head, my calendar, and my wallet. Make me a new creation. Rebuild and renew my life. Put in me a new season for Your praise and glory. I want to give as much of myself as I can to as much of You as I can understand. In Jesus' name I pray. Amen.

The Bottom Line
- Our Christian culture tends to teach that we own our money and should give some of it back to God.
- God owns everything and calls us to be stewards of 100 percent of our money.
- Being a steward is an attitude, a way of looking at life as a caretaker.
- It is not enough to give Jesus your heart, your head, and your calendar; you must also give Him control over your money.

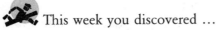 This week you discovered ...
- how to face the challenge of becoming a Biblical Christian in today's world.
- trusting Jesus not only saves you, but is supposed to change your heart, mind, calendar, and wallet.

What does God want you to do in response to this week's study?

_____

Recite 2 Corinthians 5:17 as a closing thought for the week.

---

[1]Patrick Morley, *The Man in the Mirror* (Nashville: Thomas Nelson, 1992) 138.

RESTORING RELATIONSHIPS

At the office I can always tell if someone's phone call relates to a task problem or a relationship problem. If it is a task problem, the person picks up the phone, talks for three minutes, then hangs up, smiling—mission accomplished.

If it is a relationship problem, the person answers the phone and soon his shoulders begin to slump. Keep watching and you will see a deep furrow slowly spread across his forehead. You can feel the weight of the call, even though you're not in on the details. Thirty minutes later the person slowly replaces the receiver in the cradle, heaves a deep sigh, and looks around for an aspirin bottle.

The difference between solving a task problem and a relationship problem is about 27 minutes, depending on how badly the relationship has deteriorated.

Of all the areas that suffer from poor choices, the one area that suffers most is our relationships. Even though we get into right relationship with God through recommitment, we are not automatically in right relationship with one another. The second most important thing to God is that we get into right relationship with one another.

Jesus put it this way: "A new command I give you: Love one another. As I have loved you, so you must love one another" (John 13:34). After saying the greatest commandment is to love God, Jesus said, "And the second is like it: 'Love your neighbor as yourself'" (Matthew 22:39).

On this journey we make some poor choices. The lingering effects of our poor choices are most keenly felt at the point of our relationships. It is also the most difficult area to rebuild; a broken relationship is not easily repaired. Once faith and trust have been broken, the road back is rocky. Wounded loved ones end up feeling bruised and hurt. It takes a tender, sensitive, loving man to restore a relationship.

As we get closer to the center of our lives, the stakes become greater if we create broken relationships. The nucleus of our relationships is the family. With this in mind, this week we will focus on family relationships. We will explore how:

- Biblical love is the foundation for restoring relationships.
- A tender man *initiates healing.*
- A tender man *listens attentively.*
- A tender man *expresses remorse* and *seeks forgiveness.*
- A tender man *perseveres* when reconciliation is not *immediate.*

Pray that God will keep you open and sensitive to being the kind of man God can use to bring love and forgiveness into relationships. Allow God's Spirit to convict you and give you the courage to restore relationships that need to be restored.

★ DAY 1 ★
A Tender
Man's Love

★ DAY 2 ★
Initiate
Healing

★ DAY 3 ★
Listen
Attentively

★ DAY 4 ★
Express
Remorse
and Seek
Forgiveness

★ DAY 5 ★
Persevere
and Avoid
Future
Conflict

Memorize and meditate on the following Scripture:

"Therefore, if you are offering your gift at the altar and there remember that your brother has something against you, leave your gift there in front of the altar. First go and be reconciled to your brother; then come and offer your gift" (Matthew 5:23-24).

A TENDER MAN'S LOVE

Each day when you arrive home, your wife and kids hear a first signal that you are about to reenter their orbit. Maybe it's the sound of your tires squealing on the driveway, the garage door going up, a barking dog, or the door slamming shut as you step inside.

Briefly describe your regular routine when you come home from work. How do your wife and children react to you when you come home? Is your homecoming a time of great joy, or does your family not know what to expect? Do you bring life, love, and encouragement home with you?

_____

_____

If you have made poor choices in the past, you may be experiencing hurt, brokenness, and pain in your relationships with family members and others. The first thing you must do is identify "who" and "what." *Who* have you hurt without restoring the relationship? Secondly, *what* was done that was hurtful?

List up to three persons and the hurtful actions that have caused a break in your relationship with them. There may be more than one hurt in each relationship. Do not go into detail. Simply write a brief phrase that describes the hurt(s).

Persons	Hurts
_____	_____
_____	_____
_____	_____

◆

**It is a supreme act of courage to restore your relationships
by demonstrating the love of Jesus Christ.**

While our one word of "love" has a multitude of meanings, in Scripture, different Greek words describe specific aspects of love. For example, *philos* is brotherly love, the kind of love that draws people together who are seeking a common goal. *Eros* is physical love, sexual intimacy with your mate.

The kind of love we need to restore broken relationships is *agape*, or moral love. *Agape* love demonstrates responsibility and commitment. It is unconditional love that seeks the best for the other person. This biblical love is rooted in God. "We know and rely on the love [*agape*] God has for us. God is love [*agape*]. Whoever lives in love lives in God, and God in him" (1 John 4:16).

Think of one of your relationships that most needs God's restoring and reconciling love. Below is a checklist from 1 Corinthians 13. Check the qualities of love (*agape*) that you need to demonstrate in order to restore this relationship.

❑ Patient
❑ Not rude
❑ Persevering
❑ Hopeful
❑ Protective
❑ Trusting
❑ Kind

❑ Not boastful, prideful, or arrogant
❑ Does not delight in the other's mistakes
❑ Keeps no record of wrongs
❑ Not envious or jealous
❑ Not easily angered
❑ Not self-seeking

Are you willing to work on loving this person by implementing these qualities? If you are not willing, will you allow God to work in you to make you willing?

When will you start working on restoring this relationship?_____

To whom will you be accountable for following through with restoring this relationship? _____

Jesus teaches that our love for one another should be the foundation for all relationships. Read three of the many passages that record what Jesus says about loving others and restoring relationships. Underline a key word or phrase in each one.

"Husbands, love your wives, just as Christ loved the church and gave himself for her" (Ephesians 5:25).

"Greater love has no one than this, that he lay down his life for his friends" (John 15:13).

"You have heard that it was said, 'Love your neighbor and hate your enemy.' But I tell you: Love your enemies and pray for those who persecute you" (Matthew 5:43-44).

This week we will explore how to become tender and kind men who can restore and heal relationships. A tender man filled with God's love (*agape*) has four basic characteristics:
1. A tender man *initiates healing.*
2. A tender man *listens attentively.*
3. A tender man *expresses remorse* and *seeks forgiveness.*
4. A tender man *perseveres* when reconciliation is not immediate.

At the core of *agape* is a willingness to forgive. Remember that God offered forgiveness to us through the cross before we ever asked. If you are waiting for the other person in a hurting relationship to come to you, you may have to wait forever. Tomorrow, we will explore more deeply this issue of initiating healing.

Right now, examine your heart.

Evaluate how forgiving you are. Put an x on the bar to indicate where you are right now in your life.

It's difficult for me to forgive.				I forgive others readily.

It's difficult for me to   I am able to let go of
forget past hurts.   painful memories.

I hold grudges.   I don't hold grudges.

I try to get even when   I don't seek revenge
someone hurts me.   when hurt.

God's love begins to grow when we are willing to forgive others and accept His forgiveness. If loving and forgiving others when you are hurt is difficult for you, ask God in prayer to give you the willingness to restore relationships in your life. If God is restoring relationships in your life right now, write a prayer thanking Him.

_____

_____

What does God want you to do as a result of today's study?

_____

The Bottom Line
- If you have made poor choices in the past, you may be experiencing hurt, brokenness, and pain in your relationships with family members and others.
- It is a supreme art of courage to restore your relationships by demonstrating the love of Jesus Christ.
- The kind of love we need to restore broken relationships is *agape,* or moral love.

INITIATE HEALING

A man's daughter away at college started living with a boy. It drove her father crazy. He cut her off financially and was so angry that he wouldn't speak to her. Their relationship continued to deteriorate. He was deeply offended by what she did and embarrassed too. He took it as a slap in the face of all the upbringing he had poured into her life. Later, after he cooled down, while he didn't approve of her behavior, he did long to give her a hug and say, "I love you." Yet, his pride was wounded, so he did nothing.

How do you suppose this broken relationship affected this man and his daughter spiritually?

◆

The Bible says reconciliation should precede worship.

If we have broken relationships, the Scriptures command us to go and be reconciled first—before we worship. Said another way, we cannot worship God acceptably if we are at odds with someone.

Our key verses for this week are from Matthew 5:23-24. "Therefore, if you are offering your gift at the altar and there remember that your brother has something against you, leave your gift there in front of the altar. First go and be reconciled to your brother; then come and offer your gift" (Matthew 5:23-24).

Notice the verses in Matthew 5 do not give regard to who is at fault. Your wife may erroneously hold something against you. You think she's wrong. It doesn't matter if you are right or think you are in the right. God says, "Go and be reconciled."

When there is a problem between you and another person, what keeps you from immediately going and restoring the relationship? Check the things from the list on the next page that most stand in the way of your restoring broken or strained relationships.

❑ Anger
❑ Past hurt that is now bitterness
❑ Pride
❑ Fear of rejection
❑ Reluctance to surface old problems
❑ Feeling *they* should initiate reconciliation
❑ Frustration
❑ Being hurt again and again by the same thing
❑ Feeling that restoration does no good
❑ Other: _____

How do you feel about initiating healing when the other person purposely hurt you and is unwilling to come ask forgiveness, or initiate reconciliation? Check the statements you identify with.

❑ I'm angry.   ❑ I'm unwilling if they are unwilling.
❑ I will try even if rejected.   ❑ I will ignore them.
❑ I will try to get someone else to talk to that person for me.
❑ Other: _____

Biblical love, *agape,* is unconditional. It requires you to love first, in spite of the other person's response. You are not responsible for the other person's actions. Even if he or she refuses to respond, you still have the responsibility to love, forgive, and initiate healing.

You will find strength to do this as you imitate Christ's example. His entire life—all of His actions and reactions—expressed *agape* love.

Are you willing to initiate healing with another person even if they reject you or refuse to respond? If you are, that's genuine *agape.* Forget about what others expect or how they may respond. The Bible says we must love others as Christ loved us.

But where do we start?

What do you first say to a person with whom you are seeking to restore a relationship? Often those first words are the most difficult to formulate. Knowing what to say in every circumstance is impossible. We must rely on God's Spirit and grace to help us. But certain lead-off statements could be helpful.

Circle the dot by the statements that you use or might use to initiate healing.

- "I know we are both hurting in this relationship. What can we do and say to restore this relationship?"
- "I want you to know I am sorry. Will your forgive me for _____?"
- "I would like this relationship to heal. I want to listen and will not interrupt you. Will you talk to me about the problem?"

Remember, what matters is that an unreconciled relationship is not right—it is sin. If you know a relationship isn't good or healthy, whether you were right or wrong, you must initiate reconciliation. And all the more if you know you are in the wrong. It takes a tender man to initiate healing a tender relationship. Is there someone with whom you need to initiate healing?

Will you begin praying for God's wisdom right now? Write a prayer asking God for the courage and love to initiate healing.

_____

_____

The Bottom Line
- The Bible says that reconciliation should precede worship.
- We cannot worship God acceptably if we are at odds with someone.
- Biblical love, *agape*, is unconditional.

LISTEN ATTENTIVELY

Philippians 2:4 tells us that, in following Christ's example and expressing *agape* love, we are to look not only to our own interests, but also to the interests of others. This is crucial in restoring relationships, and one way we accomplish it is by giving another person the right to speak, and then listening attentively to what he or she has to say.

Check the two or three most common feelings you have when someone takes the time and makes the effort to listen to you attentively.

❑ Respected   ❑ Important   ❑ Worthwhile
❑ Recognized   ❑ Loved   ❑ Cared for

If you have these feelings, then you know how others feel when you listen attentively to them.

◆

**Listening is the oil that lubricates the process of
restoring relationships.**

Just 20 months after Stephen's father died, Stephen's mother became deathly ill. In the days that followed, 8 of her 9 children came to pay their last respects. One daughter, however, underestimated how serious her mother's condition had become.

Every day Stephen's mother asked about her daughter, "Has anybody called her? Does she know I'm sick?" She had nightmares because her daughter didn't come. Finally, she passed away. Her daughter never came. Stephen said, "I was filled with so much anger toward my sister that I could not pray and be healed."

Over the years other offenses had built up too. You could cut the family tension with a knife. Two of his sisters had the idea to convene a weekend family gathering to hash things out. All the brothers and sisters found the idea agreeable, and they set a date.

After starting with a meal together, they were given the chance to say whatever was on their minds—how much they hurt and why, and how others had made them feel. There were some emotions, some anger, and some shouting, but nothing out of control.

They listened carefully to each other. Each felt led to apologize, express remorse, and forgive each other. Their gathering became a healing weekend that brought the family back together again.

To rebuild relationships requires active listening. How does a doctor heal the body? By asking questions and listening attentively to the patient. He cannot heal without careful listening.

The Bible emphasizes the importance of listening to one another and offers instructions about listening. Read the following passages and underline key words or phrases that speak to you.

"Let the wise listen and add to their learning, and let the discerning get guidance" (Proverbs 1:5).

"He who answers before listening—that is his folly and shame" (Proverbs 18:13).

"My dear brothers, take note of this: Everyone should be quick to listen, slow to speak and slow to become angry" (James 1:9).

When we listen to others, we should act in ways to convey that we are being attentive to what the other person is saying. Here's a list of actions. Check the two that you notice the most when you are talking to another person.

_____ Makes frequent eye contact

_____ Doesn't interrupt

_____ Remains calm

_____ Responds in a kind and gentle way

_____ Doesn't move around in an agitated way

Review the following list of pointers for listening attentively.
- Make frequent eye contact with the other person.
- Have a pleasant look on your face.
- When he or she pauses, paraphrase what you heard being said. For example, "What I hear you saying is ..."

- If you pick up feelings he or she does not articulate, you might say, "I sense you are feeling …"
- Don't interrupt or defend yourself.
- Once he or she is finished, express your feelings in "I" messages; do not project blame or accusations on the person. For example, "I feel" or "I think."

In order to be reconciled, you must understand the other person's point of view. He may not be acting rationally, but there are reasons why he does what he does.

Listening takes effort and a desire to hear completely what the other person is feeling and thinking. You are not required to agree with them, only listen.

We listen because God is a listening God. He promises to listen to us whenever we talk to Him. I challenge you to go to someone with whom you have a wounded relationship and tell him or her you are there to listen.

Who is a person to whom you need to listen? _____ Pray for the healing of that relationship. Meet with the person. Ask God to help you listen attentively.

What else does God want you to do as a result of today's study?

The Bottom Line
- Listening is the oil that lubricates the process of restoring relationships.
- In order to be reconciled, you must understand the other person's point of view.
- Listening takes effort and a desire to hear completely what the other person is feeling and thinking.

EXPRESS REMORSE AND SEEK FORGIVENESS

If your wife has asked you for years to help with small chores around the house and for years you have given her a hard time, she harbors resentment against you for not being a team player.

If you decide because of reading this material or for some other reason that you have not done right by her and want to set things straight, how would you go about it? Would you tell her, "I'm sorry," and expect everything to turn out right?

I'm sorry and *I forgive you* are key words in healing any relationship. However, to be sorry is enough to begin healing, but it is not enough to finish the job. When we hurt somebody the same way over and over again, each additional offense adds another brick to a wall building up between us. However big or small the wall, that wall represents a history.

To bring down the walls between us, we must initiate healing, listen attentively, and allow the offended person to express their grievances, anger, hurt, and pain. Then we must express genuine remorse or regret.

The biblical word that applies here is *repentance* which means to change direction and turn the other way.

◆

When we truly repent, we not only say we are sorry, but our actions change as well.

Look at the following verses and describe what they tell you about the relationship between repentance and the actions that follow it.

"Produce fruit in keeping with repentance" (Luke 3:8).

"I preached that they should repent and turn to God and prove their repentance by their deeds" (Acts 26:20).

_____

_____

These verses specifically deal with repentance as it applies to our relationship with God, but the concept is true for all relationships.

For remorse to be sincere, we must make a pledge to change. Without a willingness to change, there is no evidence of true remorse or repentance. Is there someone to whom you need to express true remorse?

If you have decided to love, forgive, ask forgiveness, and are willing to initiate healing and listen, consider the following steps.

Name the person with whom you are reconciling: _____

Describe how you will say you are sorry and ask for forgiveness.

_____

Luke 19 tells of a tax collector named Zaccheus who had become wealthy by cheating and taking advantage of many people. His meeting with Jesus prompted him to try to restore his relationships with those he had offended. He was willing to pay back four times the amount he had taken from anyone. Are you willing to go to those lengths to reconcile with someone you have offended?

Healing and acceptance of your apology may not be immediate. Hurt and pain that have built up in a relationship for months or even years may not dissipate right away. Be patient.

Reconciliation is a two-way street. Until someone says, "I'm truly sorry. Please forgive me." there is a stalemate. Until the offended party says, "I forgive you," healing can't take place. Jesus said, "If your brother sins, rebuke him, and if he repents, forgive him. If he sins against you seven times in a day, and seven times comes back to you and says, 'I repent,' forgive him" (Luke 17:3-4). You may be suffering through a relationship that is broken because you've been hurt, and you refuse to forgive.

Our relationship with God depends upon our willingness to forgive those who sin against us. Immediately after teaching the disciples how to pray, Jesus told them, "For if you forgive men when they sin against you, your heavenly Father will also forgive you. But if you do not forgive men their sins, your Father will not forgive your sins" (Matthew 6:14-15). Forgiving is not optional.

Think again of the person who has hurt you and whom you have not forgiven. Briefly describe what you need to do to be reconciled to that person.

_____

Review today's lesson. What was the most meaningful statement or Scripture you read?

_____

_____

Write a prayer of thanksgiving to God that His Son Jesus died for you and offered forgiveness to you before you ever asked.

_____

_____

Review your Scripture verse for the week–Matthew 5:23-24–and write it from memory below.

_____

_____

The Bottom Line
- *I'm sorry* and *I forgive you* are key words in healing any relationship.
- When we truly repent, we not only say we are sorry, but our actions change as well.

PERSEVERE AND DEAL WITH CONFLICT

A number of years ago I was talking on the phone to one of my brothers. We got into a dispute, and before I knew it, we were yelling at each other. In utter frustration I returned the phone to the receiver quite a bit more forcefully than recommended.

Later, I felt terrible over the things I had said but didn't know exactly what to do. It had been a really bad scene. After prayer, I had an idea.

I wrote a note in which I apologized and asked for his forgiveness. I loaded my family into the car, went by the bakery, and bought a box of fresh-baked chocolate chip cookies, then I drove to his apartment. Unfortunately, his car wasn't in the lot.

After knocking enough times to make sure he wasn't there, I put the note and cookies behind the screen door.

I never heard from him.

It took several years and much prayer before our relationship began to recover. That's one of the prices of hurting each other. Sometimes the wounds don't heal overnight.

◆

**A tender man will persevere when reconciliation
is not immediate.**

We cannot control the other person. We can control ourselves. We can only continue to respond in the Spirit.

Is there someone in your life that you have been seeking a healed relationship with for a long time? Are you ready to give up? Think about the limits of your patience. If you are actively working on restoring a relationship, how long would you be willing to work on it before giving up? Check one.

   ❑ a few days   ❑ a few weeks   ❑ a few months
   ❑ a year or so   ❑ a few years   ❑ a lifetime

On the other side of your perseverance is a healed relationship. Are you willing to wait? Patience is a fruit of God's Spirit (see Galatians 5:22). Mark an x on the bar that represents your perseverance with restoring relationships.

I write a person off right away   I wait indefinitely for a
when he doesn't accept   person to accept my apology.
my apology.

I try to manipulate people   I refuse to control others.
when they don't respond to
my initiatives to restore relationships.

Obviously, if we can avoid conflict in the first place, our relationships will be far better off. But conflict is part of life, so knowing how to deal with conflict is a critical part of living together.

Check the statement that best describes how you normally handle conflict.
- ❏ I simmer a long time like coals in a fire.
- ❏ I explode in anger like a firecracker.
- ❏ I become defensive.
- ❏ I go on the offensive and attack.
- ❏ I try to avoid conflict and anger at all costs.
- ❏ I dig up the past and throw it at the other person.
- ❏ I handle conflict with maturity.

Some time ago our kids, like all kids, were fighting too much in the mornings getting ready for school. My reaction to all of this was the typical male overreaction, which got us nowhere. Finally, I figured the best thing I could do was to sort out my thoughts and feelings in writing, and then have a family meeting to see if we could iron things out calmly.

Listed on the following page are some suggestions I wrote down during this incident. Underline the ones you need to work on.

- Pray for and act out a Christlike attitude. Ask yourself, "What would Jesus do?"
- Don't expect to always get what you want. Families and friends must give and take.
- Don't be petty. Let offenses go.
- Be more concerned about the relationship than getting your way.
- Relationships are usually more important than being right.
- Don't lose your temper; it doesn't bring about the righteous life God desires.

I also suggested some healthy ways to resolve conflict. Think of a relationship right now that contains hurt and conflict. Check the step that would be most helpful for you.

❏ Refuse to lose your temper. Talk calmly and kindly.
❏ Try counting to ten.
❏ Try walking away, suggesting you discuss it after you cool down.
❏ Don't attack the other *person*; stay focused on the *issue*.
❏ Don't try to hurt the other person intentionally.
❏ Talk about what you want to happen and your own feelings.
❏ Try to understand the other person's point of view.
❏ Be quick to apologize.

When my family implemented these suggestions, the entire tone of our mornings changed. The best way to enjoy healthy relationships is to avoid the hurt that comes with conflict. Developing a plan of action helps us do that.

Write your suggestions for how you can avoid unnecessary conflict, and how you can deal positively with it when it does occur.

_____

_____

It is true that relationships often take more time than tasks. It is true that relationships often cause more conflict than tasks. It is true that relationships talk back, and sometimes we have to compromise. Somehow, though, we must grasp the idea that Jesus puts the premium on relationships, not tasks. The only "new" commandment Jesus gave during His earthly ministry was that we love one another as He loved us. This love is the glue that can keep us together and the oil that can keep us from rubbing each other the wrong way.

The Bottom Line
- **Sometimes the wounds don't heal overnight.**
- **A tender man will persevere when reconciliation is not immediate.**

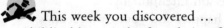 This week you discovered ...
- biblical love as the foundation for restoring wounded relationships.
- how to initiate healing.
- how to listen attentively.
- how to express remorse and seek forgiveness.
- how to persevere when reconciliation is not immediate.

What does God want you to do in response to this week's study?

_____

_____

Repeat Matthew 5:23-24 and meditate on its meaning for your life.

THREE PRIVATE SPIRITUAL DISCIPLINES

Once upon a time I was an avid fisherman. Then I caught "the big one"—a 9-pound, 13-ounce smallmouth bass. (I had it stuffed to prove I did it.) After that, fishing never turned my crank like it did before. Here's how it happened.

It was a warm, muggy Memorial Day morning. My wife and two small children took advantage of the holiday and slept in. Not me, though. I was on the lake early. Ordinarily, my little jonboat would slip across the water at the slightest breeze, but this still day, it sat like it was frozen in concrete. I hit the battery-powered trolling motor and glided another few yards around the shoreline.

I positioned myself about 50 feet from the shoreline and began to cast into all the places I would hide if I were the Loch Ness bass.

On my first pass around the lake I didn't get a single strike. I was just completing working my plastic worm in from the shoreline when I heard the water ripple slightly on the other side of my boat. Bored, I gave it a little flick of the wrist. I was surprised to see the worm land on the other side of the boat precisely where the water had rippled.

Immediately, something akin to King Kong with fins grabbed my bait and started to run. My heart stopped beating. *Could this be my day?*

Now, the number-one rule for catching bass is that you let the fish run with the bait. If you try to set the hook too soon, the bass will simply spit out the bait and, with it, the hook. Instead, you make sure the fish feels no resistance so that it will think it has the worm, no "strings" attached. You want that bass to get lulled into a false sense of confidence—to feel safe enough to swallow the whole bait. So you let it run, count to 10 or 20 real slow, then give a strong yank, and set the hook. After that, all you do is reel her in—there's no way for her to get away.

That's exactly how Satan works too. He lets us grab the bait, but he doesn't try to set the hook right away. Instead, he lets us run until we lull ourselves into a false confidence. Then, just when we are sure it's safe, he sets the hook, and it's too late. All that's left is to reel us in. Have you ever felt like Satan had you hooked? Have you had the helpless feeling of being reeled in and there was nothing you could do about it?

This week you will:
• Discover the spiritual battle you are in.
• Learn what spiritual discipline is all about.
• Understand how to approach Bible study.
• Work on developing an effective prayer life.
• Be disciplined in having a quiet time with the Lord.

★ DAY 1 ★ What Is the Battle and What Is the Discipline?	★ DAY 2 ★ The Spiritual Disciplines	★ DAY 3 ★ The Discipline of Bible Study
★ DAY 4 ★ The Discipline of Prayer	★ DAY 5 ★ The Discipline of a Quiet Time	

Memorize and meditate on the following Scripture this week.

Finally, be strong in the Lord and in his mighty power. Put on the full armor of God so that you can take your stand against the devil's schemes. For our struggle is not against flesh and blood, but against the rulers, against the authorities, against the powers of this dark world and against the spiritual forces of evil in the heavenly realms (Ephesians 6:10-12).

WHAT IS THE BATTLE AND WHAT IS THE DISCIPLINE?

We are constantly in a spiritual battle with an enemy who wants to defeat our Christian faith—an enemy who wants to distract us, discourage us, disillusion us, and defeat us. That's why the apostle Paul made frequent use of the military image: "Endure hardship with us like a good soldier of Christ Jesus" (2 Timothy 2:3).

We won't win the spiritual battle, though, if we identify it as a worldly war. The Bible says, "For our struggle is not against flesh and blood, but against the rulers, against the powers of this dark world and against the spiritual forces of evil in the heavenly realms" (Ephesians 6:12). Our enemy is the devil, and we cannot face him alone without getting slapped around.

Read the following passages and circle the word or phrase that identifies where strength and power for the battle come from.

The Lord is my light and my salvation—whom shall I fear? The Lord is the stronghold of my life—of whom shall I be afraid? (Psalm 27:1).

No, in all these things we are more than conquerors through him (Christ) who loved us (Romans 8:37-39).

"'Not by might nor by power, but my my Spirit,' says the Lord Almighty" (Zechariah 4:6).

◆

A spiritual battle can only be won with spiritual weapons.

We will never win this battle if we fight with the wrong weapons. If your dog had fleas, you wouldn't try to get rid of them with a shotgun. You wouldn't try to get the chinch bugs out of your lawn by using dynamite. You wouldn't try to repel a charging pit bull with a flyswatter.

Think about yourself for a moment. Check the worldly weapons you use most often when you don't rely on the Lord.
- ❏ Hard work
- ❏ Positive thinking
- ❏ Listening to motivational speakers and tapes
- ❏ Finding people who will encourage me and pump me up
- ❏ Making better plans and working my plans harder
- ❏ Becoming more religious and doing more religious things

Too often we try to win the daily battles we fight with worldly weapons—working harder, positive thinking, better planning, et cetera. The weapons God offers us in the Bible—the armor of God—are often referred to as "the spiritual disciplines." Many of them are referred to in Ephesians 6:13-18.

> Therefore put on the full armor of God, so that when the day of evil comes, you may be able to stand your ground and after you have done everything, to stand. Stand firm then, with the belt of truth buckled around your waist, with the breastplate of righteousness in place, and with your feet fitted with the readiness that comes from the gospel of peace. In addition to all this, take up the shield of faith, with which you can extinguish all the flaming arrows of the evil one. Take the helmet of salvation and the sword of the Spirit, which is the word of God. And pray in the Spirit on all occasions with all kinds of prayers and requests. With this in mind, be alert and always keep on praying for all the saints.

List the offensive weapons described in the previous passage. Then list the defensive parts of the armor.

_____

_____

_____

As a soldier of Jesus Christ, we have the right weapons, but we must also know how to use them effectively. That means we must regularly practice using them. We must exercise discipline.

Write your definition of discipline.

_____

_____

List three activities that require training and discipline.

1. _____

2. _____

3. _____

The Bible exhorts us to discipline ourselves to be godly. Discipline involves training, correction, learning, and exercising biblical principles. Paul wrote the key instruction about spiritual discipline:

"Have nothing to do with godless myths and old wives' tales; rather, train yourself to be godly. For physical training is of some value, but godliness has value for all things, holding promise for both the present life and the life to come" (1 Timothy 4:7-8).

We often think of training as essential for sports and for careers. But training is the avenue to excellence in any field. Most of us, though, tend not to be disciplined. In the garden of Gethsemane, Jesus told His disciples to watch and pray. When He returned, He found them asleep. He said, "The spirit is willing, but the body is weak" (Matthew 26:41). I believe there is not a man who truly knows Christ who doesn't want to walk with and please God. But, in our flesh we are weak. To overcome our weakness, we must exercise spiritual discipline. So what is the purpose of spiritual discipline? Ultimately, the Bible says we are to become like Jesus. We are to be transformed into His likeness (see 2 Corinthians 3:18; Romans 12:1-2).

Sometimes we must substitute discipline for a lack of natural interest. You may be too tired to toss a baseball with your son, but it may be exactly what you ought to do. You deny yourself and put on your glove.

In the same way, we don't always feel like emulating Jesus. Yet, we forge ahead, pick up the Bible, and study it. Spiritual discipline sometimes means: *Do what you don't want to do, and you will become what you want to be.*

We do not practice spiritual discipline to earn the love and approval of our heavenly Father. At times, you may feel God should bless or reward you because you have prayed. This is a distorted Christianity that we must overcome. We practice disciplines because we love Him and desire to be more like Him.

 Which do you tend to worry more about—your external actions or the transformation of your inner man? Put an x on the bar to represent where your focus is right now.

Doing things for Jesus　　　　Being transformed by Jesus

Our effectiveness for the kingdom of God is not based on what we can do for Jesus, but rather on what He can do in and through us. In order for us to be effective soldiers, we must be conformed to His image and likeness and be obedient to Him.

 Write a prayer telling God how you wish to be more like Christ.

The Bottom Line
- We are constantly in a spiritual battle with an enemy who wants to defeat our Christian faith—an enemy who wants to distract us, discourage us, disillusion us, and defeat us.
- Our enemy is the devil and we cannot face him alone without getting slapped around.
- A spiritual battle can only be won with spiritual weapons.

THE SPIRITUAL DISCIPLINES

If a farmer tills, plants, waters, and harvests but never puts anything back into the soil, eventually, the soil will give out. In the same way, the believer needs to put something back into his relationship with God. The spiritual disciplines are the means by which we keep our relationship with the Lord alive and growing.

Spiritual disciplines allow us to be connected to God moment-by-moment in personal relationship. A strong relationship with anyone correlates to the amount of time and energy invested in the relationship.

◆

The spiritual disciplines help us build a vital, moment-by-moment relationship with Christ.

How close is your relationship with the Lord? Mark with an x on each bar to indicate where you are in the following areas.

Distant from the Lord   Close to the Lord

Disciplined in my spiritual life   Undisciplined

Prepared for whatever battles I may face   Unprepared

Where you rated yourself will help you determine how much you may need to build or rebuild the vitality of your relationship with Christ.

Spiritual disciplines are *gifts*, not *requirements*. They are *graces*, not *laws*. You may think, *Oh no, not another list of things to do!* The spiritual disciplines are not simply more things to do. They are not a series of duties or mechanical steps to perform by rote.

Spiritual disciplines are means, not ends. They have no value in and of themselves. They offer the practitioner no spiritual superiority over someone else.

Spiritual disciplines do not save us. We attain no merit for our salvation through our works or sufferings. Salvation is the free gift of God by faith. Spiritual disciplines, though, are the means to pursue godliness in response to our salvation, but not to gain any merit or advance any cause.

The Christian walk is a beautiful journey when we walk Christ's way. Walk it any other way, and it can be a desperate thing. Christ has given us great freedom. Freedom in Christ, though, is the liberty to do what we *ought* to do rather than what we *want* to do.

There are historic spiritual disciplines that have become the tried, tested, and proven means of grace through which God makes Himself known to us. By understanding and employing these disciplines, we follow God's plan for us, gain weapons for the spiritual battles we will fight, and gain the temporal blessings God desires to give us.

Private spiritual disciplines can be divided into inward and outward disciplines. Inward private disciplines include prayer, meditation, study, journaling, fasting, silence, and singing. Outward private disciplines include withdrawal, engagement, simplicity, service, solitude, evangelism, submission, stewardship, accountability, chastity, spiritual direction, secrecy, affirmation, sacrifice, and watching.[1]

Notice the variety of spiritual disciplines. Think of them as conduits, pipelines, or roads to get in touch with God. You will not use them all, most likely—at least not all the time. When you want to get in touch with someone, you can phone, send a fax, a letter, an express mail letter, EMAIL, or a messenger. In the same way, the spiritual disciplines are many different ways to help us communicate with and worship God.

Different disciplines have different levels of importance—call it a hierarchy of importance. Obviously, Bible study, worship, and prayer are generally more important than, say, journaling or silence.

Spiritual disciplines are *spiritual exercises* that help us become more like Jesus. They help us attain godly character.

In particular, we are going to look at three disciplines I consider crucial to every man's training to be like Christ. Circle your feelings about being involved in the disciplines of *prayer*, *Bible study*, or *quiet time*.

Burdened	Joyful	Relaxed	Liberated
Excited	Frustrated	Expectant	Bored

If you are burdened by these spiritual disciplines, step back and think prayerfully about the Psalm 42:1 for the next few days.

As the deer pants for streams of water,
   so my soul pants for you, O God.
My soul thirsts for God, for the living God.
   When can I go and meet with God? (Psalm 42:1).

Pray that God would give you a hunger to meet with Him.

Evaluate where you are in relation to the three private inward disciplines we will study the next three days. Shade each of the bars below to the level of your commitment to these three disciplines:

Bible Study

Low		Medium		High

Prayer

Low		Medium		High

Quiet Time

Low		Medium		High

[1]These disciplines represent a synthesis of those mentioned in three books I recommend for further study: Richard Foster, *Celebration of Discipline* (San Francisco: Harper and Row, 1978); Dallas Willard, *The Spirit of the Disciplines* (San Francisco: Harper Collins, 1988); and Donald Whitney, *Spiritual Disciplines for the Christian Life* (Colorado Springs: NavPress, 1991).

The Bottom Line
- The spiritual disciplines are the means by which we keep our relationship with the Lord alive and growing.
- The spiritual disciplines help us build a vital, moment-by-moment relationship with Christ.
- Spiritual disciplines are the means to pursue godliness in response to our salvation, but not to gain any merit or advance any cause.

THE DISCIPLINE OF BIBLE STUDY

On the Via Dolorosa in the Old City of Jerusalem, the significance of a nondescript store run by Ferridah Hana could easily be lost amid the menagerie of garish hawkers stationed along that historic road. I met Ferridah Hana on a pilgrimage to the Holy Land.

Known as the Mother Teresa of Israel, this Arab Christian, Ferridah Hana, supports 600 orphans out of her tiny shop. From her income she has started two orphanages and a children's hospital. In her store she sells love beads, so named because it can take a little disabled child an entire day to put a single bead on the string. She also takes in abandoned Muslim widows without families and teaches them to sew for a living.

One day she was sitting in her store visiting with two American men. Into her shop came two other Americans, rude men who talked loudly about how filthy the Arabs were in that quarter of the Old City, not knowing Ferridah, whose shop is spotless, was an Arab.

One of her American visitors began to get up to give his rude fellow countrymen a piece of his mind. Ferridah reached over, put her hand on his shoulder, and gently pressed him to sit back down. Then she said, "You Americans are so interesting. You take your Bible literally, but you don't take it seriously."

◆

**A man's life will never change in any significant way
apart from the regular study of God's Word.**

The Bible is God speaking to man. The Bible communicates the truth of God to men in search of ultimate reality. *The God who is* is revealed in Scripture. The Bible, then, is the starting point of a life with God. He is rich who dwells upon God's Word. Psalm 19:7-11 says:

The law of the Lord is perfect,
    reviving the soul.
The statutes of the Lord are trustworthy,
    making wise the simple.
The precepts of the Lord are right,
    giving joy to the heart.

The commands of the Lord are radiant,
  giving light to the eyes. The fear of the Lord is pure,
  enduring forever.
The ordinances of the Lord are sure
  and altogether righteous.
They are more precious than gold,
  than much pure gold;
they are sweeter than honey,
  than honey from the comb.
By them is your servant warned;
  in keeping them there is great reward.

One way to study the Bible is to mark a passage when you read it. For example, look over Psalm 19:7-11 *in your own Bible* and...

Put a question mark (?) wherever there is a word or phrase that you do not understand and need to study further at a later time.

Put an arrow (→) each place the passage goes directly to your heart and is particularly meaningful to you.

Underline those parts that you want to remember or memorize.

Systematic study helps you learn and remember God's Word. Here are some ways you might systematically study. Check the ways you use the most and circle one you would be willing to try in the next few weeks.

_____ Read through a book of the Bible. Read one paragraph or chapter each day. Outline the book as you read.

_____ Study a doctrine or theme of Scripture such as grace, love, salvation, sin, or faith. Use a concordance to track that word through various books of the Bible.

_____ Pick a biblical character (like Abraham, Moses, David, Ruth, Mary, or Paul) and do a biographical study highlighting the lessons that person learned in his or her relationship to the Lord.

_____ Participate in a weekly Bible study with a group of men who are serious about learning God's Word. Use one of the approaches already listed as your basis of study.

A friend in the publishing business tells me that only 30 percent of college graduates ever read a book after graduation. Reading and studying have largely been replaced by watching television and videos. For the Christian, however, reading and study open the door to communication from God.

Frankly, after more than 20 years of following Christ, I find I no longer read my Bible. My Bible reads me. On its crinkly pages I see myself—my motives, my ambitions, my longings, my pain, my suffering, my sins, my hope, my joy. As the rustling pages turn, I see God— His love, His forgiveness, His birth, His death, His resurrection, His sovereignty, His holiness, His character.

As you examine your own study habits, rate from 1 (I most need) to 5 (I'm OK) what you need to spend more time and effort doing as you study God's Word.

____ read the Word
____ study the meaning of books, doctrines, and biblical principles
____ apply the Word in my daily life
____ teach the Word in my family
____ become part of a Bible study group
____ memorize and meditate on Scriptures
____ learn the background and meaning of the Scriptures

What does God want you to do in response to today's study?

The Bottom Line
- A man's life will never change in any significant way apart from the regular study of God's Word.
- The Bible, then, is the starting point of a life with God.
- For the Christian, however, reading and study open the door to communication from God.

THE DISCIPLINE OF PRAYER

One day I was trying to decide if I should send a copy of a letter I received from President Clinton to our ministry partners list. It didn't feel right. I talked it over with a man in our office but couldn't get closure. As I was concluding the conversation, I said, "Well, I'll keep praying about it." Just then it hit me that I had been thinking about it, but not actually praying. There is a huge difference being thinking and praying. I prayed and immediately the answer came—don't send it.

When a friend of mine became deathly ill with cancer, another friend asked me how he was doing. "He's a very sick boy," I said. "I guess the only thing we can do is pray."

"No," he corrected. "The thing we *can* do is pray." What gave his statement added authority was that he offered this advice just 6 months after his wife of 26 years had died from cancer.

◆

Prayer should be the first thing we do, not the last.

Why don't we pray more? First, we pray last or don't pray at all because we don't believe prayer *really* works. If we *really* believed God hears and answers prayers, we would pray all the time. If we really understood prayer, it would be the principal habit of our hearts. It would be our first resort, not our last.

Second, prayer is hard work. One day I was in the car with Bill and Vonette Bright. At the time Vonette was the chair of the National Day of Prayer—she even got Congress to make it a law! I nearly ran off the road when she said, "Prayer is hard work. Sometimes I find it hard to concentrate. My mind wanders." Well, I already knew that was true for me! I just couldn't believe it was true for one of the world's most famous pray-ers! What an encouragement! Prayer *is* hard work.

When you have a difficult time praying, what distracts you? Check your two or three most common distractions.

- ❏ Problems
- ❏ Doubt
- ❏ Lack of time
- ❏ Worry
- ❏ Boredom

- ❏ Finances
- ❏ Uncertainty in how to pray
- ❏ Ignorance of the Word
- ❏ Disappointment from earlier prayers
- ❏ Other _____

Prayer changes us. Prayer breaks strongholds. Prayer determines the destinies of men, their families, their communities, and their nations. Only an army of men on their knees can turn the destiny of America back to God. It's time for you to get on your knees and fight like a man! What is your prayer life like? Is prayer a significant part of your life? Do you sense a close, personal communion with Jesus when you pray? Or is your prayer life more limited, mechanical, and unrewarding? Here are a few suggestions.

Use catchwords. If your prayer life is in a rut, you might consider one of the things that helps me—catchwords. I have these words written in the front of my Bible. When I pray during my daily quiet time, I let my eyes stop on each word and see if it triggers something to pray over. It keeps my prayer life fresh and focused.

For example, one of my catchwords is *comfort.* One day when I see this word, it brings to mind how hard yesterday was when that deal fell apart. Another day it brings to mind Jesus saying to me, "Come to me, all you who are weary and burdened, and I will give you rest" (Matthew 11:28). Another time I am overwhelmed by a sense of God's love and peace welling up in my chest through the Holy Spirit.

Here is a partial list of catchwords I use (no order implied):

- objectivity, truth, no self-deceit
- worship, praise, love, trust, glorify, enjoy
- impure thoughts, selfish ambitions, wrong motives, unrealistic expectations
- negative attitudes, hurtful words, touchy feeling, critical spirit
- insight, wisdom, guidance, vision
- comfort, rest, fellowship, encouragement, healing
- power, life change, sanctification
- strength, courage, hope, grace, mercy
- humility, obedience, fear of the Lord
- will of God, calling, gifts

- creativity, imagination, passion, excellence, integrity
- filled/walk in Spirit, grateful, joyful, faithful, available, teachable
- consecrated, unhardened heart, servant
- dependent, not self-reliant, abide, delight, disengaged
- safety, blessing, promises

Why don't you stop and pray a prayer using some of the key words I have suggested? Consider writing catchwords of your own in your Bible or daily planner.

Write down prayers. Pray with a pencil in your hand. By writing down prayer requests you get to see God working. It's amazing how often I forget to thank God for answering requests I don't write down.

In the front of my Bible, I have written my specific long-term prayer requests. These include important people in my life—saved and un-saved—and different projects.

For short-term prayer items I use removable notes and stick them in blank spaces next to my long-term requests.

If you don't already write down your prayers, why not give it a try? Then you can be sure to praise God for His answers.

Take a moment, write down requests you have made of God recently. List any answers you have received. Come back to this page later and write down any answers God gives.

Prayer Request	Answer from God
_____	_____
_____	_____
_____	_____

Pray Scripture. One way to connect with the Lord is to repeat His Word to Him in prayer. Some passages of Scripture naturally lend themselves to prayer such as the Lord's Prayer in Matthew 6, Psalm 51, 139, or 23.

Choose one of the following Scriptures and say it as a prayer to God: Ephesians 3:16-21; 1 Corinthians 13; Psalm 91; Psalm 30; Psalm 86.

Pray with a partner. The Bible encourages us to pray with one another, "I tell you that if two of you on earth agree about anything you ask for, it will be done for you by my Father in heaven. For where two or three come together in my name, there am I with them" (Matthew 18:19-20).

 List three people you could ask to pray with you—either as a one-time experience or, if so led, as a regular prayer partner.

God wants us to pray. Prayer is man speaking to God. Prayer is how we communicate with God. Prayer changes things. However, God doesn't answer petitions that are not presented. If we go about solving our challenges in our own strength, we rob God of the glory He wants for Himself. He would rather we come humbly before the throne of His grace so that He can give us mercy and help in our times of need.

What does God want you to do as a result of today's study?

The Bottom Line
- Prayer should be the first thing we do, not the last.
- We pray last or don't pray at all because we don't believe prayer really works.
- Prayer is hard work.
- Prayer determines the destinies of men, their families, their communities, and their nations.
- Only an army of men on their knees can turn the destiny of America back to God.

THE DISCIPLINE OF A QUIET TIME

In our culture we have a device called "quiet time."

◆

**A quiet time is a routine period of time set aside
for meeting with God.**

Many people set aside 15, 30 minutes, or an hour or more daily to read and study God's Word, pray, and possibly perform some other spiritual disciplines. For example, sometimes I like to sing hymns (it's the only place I dare to!), journal, or read devotional materials.

The Bible calls for continual prayer and meditation: "Pray continually" (1 Thessalonians 5:17); "Pray in the Spirit on all occasions with all kinds of prayers and requests" (Ephesians 6:18); "His delight is in the law of the Lord, and on his law he meditates day and night" (Psalm 1:2).

The quiet time, then, is an accommodation to an overly busy culture. Nevertheless, the concept of setting aside a regular time to be with the Lord will greatly enhance any man's walk with God.

When is the best time for you to have your quiet time? Look at your daily schedule and write your first and second choices below.

First choice: _____ Second choice: _____

Why is it important to have a quiet time? A fundamental principle of our national defense policy is that we defend against *capabilities,* not *intentions.* Enemies say one thing and do another. We can't trust Satan's lies. He wants to destroy you.

Each day we must resupply ourselves for the spiritual battle. To run out of spiritual food, ammunition, and strength can be catastrophic.

What does the Bible say about spending time with God? Read the following passages and briefly write what each passage teaches.

Be still, and know that I am God   _____
(Psalm 46:10).   _____

Come near to God and he will come near
to you (James 4:8).

_____

_____

Come to me, all you who are weary and
burdened, and I will give you rest. Take my
yoke upon you and learn from me, for I am
gentle and humble in heart, and you will
find rest for your souls (Matthew 11:28-30).

_____

_____

_____

_____

_____

How much time should you devote to a daily quiet time? If you don't already have a quiet time, consider giving five minutes a day to read one chapter of the New Testament and say a prayer such as the Lord's Prayer. Later, if you want to increase the time you spend, fine. But start with a realistic goal. *The best length of time is the one you will actually do.* Don't bite off more than you will really do.

In Yosemite Park you can see grass growing out of the rocks up high. A tiny seed, by applying consistent pressure, works its roots into the rock and finds life. No matter how hard your circumstances, if you apply consistent pressure and have a daily quiet time, those roots will take hold for you.

How often should you have a quiet time? Shoot for five days a week, allowing for such things as early morning meetings and glitches. You wouldn't expect to eat once or twice a week and be healthy. Neither can you feed your spirit once or twice a week and expect spiritual health.

Another idea for your quiet time is to spend time with your wife in Bible study, sharing, and prayer. Many women cannot understand why their husbands will not read the Bible and pray with them. Most men who do have a quiet time of their own fail to share spiritually with their wives. The same is also true for a family time of spiritual sharing together. The husband has a responsibility to be a spiritual leader in the marriage and family (see Ephesians 5).

What's your plan for your quiet time? Write down a realistic commitment and then pray that the Holy Spirit will give you the desire, time, and willingness to spend a consistent quiet time with Him.

My Quiet Time with God

How often? _____

What time? _____

My quiet time will include:
❑ Scripture Reading   ❑ Prayer   ❑ Other:_____

My Prayer of Commitment

_____

_____

The Bottom Line
- A quiet time is a routine period of time set aside for meeting with God.
- The Bible calls for continual prayer and meditation.
- Each day we must resupply ourselves for the spiritual battle. To run out of spiritual food, ammunition, and strength can be catastrophic.
- The best length of time is the one you will actually do.

This week you discovered ...
- the importance of maintaining private spiritual disciplines.
- how to approach Bible study.
- how to have an effective prayer life.
- how to maintain a daily quiet time with the Lord.

What does God want you to do in response to this week's study?

_____

Recite Ephesians 6:10-12 from memory and meditate on it the remainder of today.

THREE PUBLIC SPIRITUAL DISCIPLINES

Many men in our society get caught up in the daily grind of unthinking routines. If we are not careful, we can find ourselves living shallow and often meaningless lives. Ours is an anonymous, dangerous age.

One of the greatest losses to men in this generation has been the privatization of our faith. We have been taught that faith is personal, a private thing. We have been taught to separate our public life from our private faith.

As a result, men often walk their spiritual walk alone. They don't have any Christian friends, at least below the level of news, sports, and weather. So they become vulnerable to failure.

A man cannot be successful by himself.

A man can be successful only when he lives in community. Public spiritual disciplines done in community keep us from falling prey to the sins of anonymity. There are many public disciplines, but for this week we will limit our discussion to three potent ones: the accountability group, Bible studies, and church.

During the next week you will:
- Discover how to be accountable in a small group of Christian men;
- Uncover two important reasons why men don't have more accountability for their private lives;
- Realize the tremendous value of ongoing Bible study with other men;
- Study the biblical meaning of church and practical ways to build community;
- Learn the importance of worship and fellowship within a body of believers.

★ DAY 1 ★
Men in
Community

★ DAY 2 ★
The Discipline
of
Accountability

★ DAY 3 ★
The Discipline
of
Bible Study

★ DAY 4 ★
The Discipline
of Church:
Worship

★ DAY 5 ★
The Discipline
of Church:
Fellowship

In preparation for this week's emphasis, memorize, meditate on, and implement these three proverbs in your life.

As iron sharpens iron,
     so one man sharpens another (Proverbs 27:17).

Plans fail for lack of counsel,
     but with many advisers they succeed (Proverbs 15:22).

Wounds from a friend can be trusted,
     but an enemy multiplies kisses (Proverbs 27:6).

MEN IN COMMUNITY

We have all known men like this ...

In the early morning darkness they migrate like lemmings from neighborhoods in which they don't know their neighbors, down impersonal expressways to catacombs of commerce where they scurry about like rats in a maze. At lunch they leave jobs in which they hardly know their coworkers to work out at a health club with other overweight men they've never met. After working late and forgetting to call home, they leave customers whose names they easily forget to arrive home after dark for a warmed-over dinner with a wife they barely know. On Sunday they arise and travel to a church with kids they never spend much time with to hear a sermon with a bunch of people whose names they have long since forgotten from a pastor to whom they've only said hello. They rush out the door to watch football games for which they will never remember the score. Their lives are thin as cardboard. They are the generation of cardboard men who live, eat, and sleep cardboard lives.

 How much of yourself do you see in this description? Are you a "lone ranger," trying to make it through life basically on your own? Or are you finding safety and strength in meaningful relationships with other men? Mark an x on the bar to show where you are right now.

Lone Ranger   Meaningful Relationships

Women move about like sheep in the safety of groups, while men wander alone like proud lions through enemy territory. But the Bible says we are all sheep, men and women alike. We think we are like the fierce lion. We are really like Mary's little lamb. To wander alone is neither wise nor safe. We all, like sheep, can go astray.

◆

**A man who walks alone is like a lost sheep
culled out from the safety of the flock by a wily wolf.**

Let's look at some of the things the Bible says we're to do with other Christians. In the following verses, underline the words "one another" or "each other."

"Be devoted to one another in brotherly love. Honor one another above yourselves" (Romans 12:10).

"Therefore, encourage one another and build each other up, just as in fact you are doing" (1 Thessalonians 5:11).

"You, my brothers, were called to be free. But do not use your freedom to indulge the sinful nature; rather, serve one another" (Galatians 5:13).

"Bear with each other and forgive whatever grievances you may have against one another" (Colossians 3:13).

"Let the word of Christ dwell in you richly as you teach and admonish one another with all wisdom, as you sing psalms, hymns and spiritual songs with gratitude in your hearts to God" (Colossians 3:16).

Now go back and circle the verbs in those verses that indicate our responsibilities and privileges within the Christian community. How many men do you relate to at this level? List their names.

_____

_____

Were there more than one or two? If not, are you willing to reach out to other Christian men to share on a deeper spiritual level in prayer, Bible study, and accountability?

If you bought into the idea that "faith is a private thing," the devil may be using this to make you vulnerable and to keep you apart from other men. Man can only be successful when he lives in community with other believers.

Review today's lesson. What was the most meaningful statement or Scripture you read?

_____

_____

Reword the statement or Scripture into a prayer response to God.

_____

_____

The Bottom Line
- A man who walks alone is like a lost sheep culled out from the safety of the flock by a wily wolf.
- To walk alone is neither wise nor safe.
- Man can only be successful when he lives in community with other believers.

THE DISCIPLINE OF ACCOUNTABILITY

Balancing priorities can be confusing. Many men don't even know what their priorities should be—much less how to balance them. Some issues in life can't be handled by self-examination and the study of God alone. Sometimes we need a friend to help us see things more clearly.

We have been led to believe we should play our cards close to the vest. Here are other words of advice from our society:

- Don't tell anyone anything that can be used against you.
- People who share their problems are weak.
- You can't depend on anyone but yourself.
- Don't let anyone know your personal business.

The truth for the Biblical Christian is: There is power in vulnerability, strength in numbers, and safety in visibility. The most successful Christians I know have some accountability built into their lives. The Bible puts it this way: "Plans fail for lack of counsel, but with many advisers they succeed" (Proverbs 15:22).

◆

Accountability means to be regularly answerable for each of the key areas in your life to qualified people.

I believe no man can stay on track with his God, his family, his friends, his morality, his money, and his vocation unless he has an accountable relationship with other men.

How do you feel about the last statement concerning accountability? Where do you feel you are most accountable and least accountable in your life? Check the areas where you have strong accountability, and put an x beside each area where you are weak.

- ❏ My relationship with God
- ❏ My relationships with friends
- ❏ My career and work habits
- ❏ My spiritual growth
- ❏ My marriage and family
- ❏ My money and stewardship
- ❏ My morality
- ❏ My use of leisure time

So why don't more men have accountability in their private lives? List three reasons you hesitate to be more accountable in your life.

_____

_____

Let's compare reasons. First, *fear.* Why are we afraid? We fear a loss of reputation. As people say, confession is good for the soul but bad for the reputation. We assume if other men know what we are really like, they won't accept us. Of course, that other man feels the same way.

Men fear betrayal. We fear that accountability will be like a powerful light shined on our blemishes. It can wound our pride.

One way we can overcome this fear is to understand the benefits of accountability described in the Bible. Read the passages below and summarize the benefits presented.

If someone is caught in a sin, you who _____
are spiritual should restore him gently. _____
But watch ... you also may be tempted. _____
Carry each other's burdens, and in this _____
way you will fulfill the law of Christ _____
(Galatians 6:1-2). _____

Confess your sins to each other and _____
pray for each other so that you may be _____
healed. The prayer of a righteous man _____
is powerful and effective (James 5:16). _____

The Lord's servant must not quarrel; _____
instead, he must be kind to everyone, _____
able to teach, not resentful. Those who _____
oppose him he must gently instruct, in _____
the hope that God will grant them _____
repentance leading them to a knowledge _____
of the truth (2 Timothy 2:24-25). _____

A second reason men are not more accountable to one another is *false confidence*. We don't think we need to be accountable. We think we can make it on our own. We think there are better uses of our time so we don't make accountability a priority. We don't realize how weak we are.

Scripture tells why accountability protects us from our weakness. Read the following verses and underline the reasons "two are better than one."

"Two are better than one, because they have a good return for their work: If anyone falls down, his friend can help him up. But pity the man who falls and has no one to help him up! ... Though one may be overpowered, two can defend themselves. A cord of three strands is not easily broken" (Ecclesiastes 4:9-10,12).

For an accountable relationship to demonstrate the success promised in the passage above, all parties involved must exhibit three specific qualities. They must be vulnerable, confidential, and confrontational. *Vulnerable* means to open up honestly. *Confidential* means you can be trusted not to tell others what's shared with you (see Proverbs 16:28). And, *confrontational* means you're willing to ask the hard questions.

The verses I shared at the beginning of the week fit perfectly into this discussion. I also added Proverbs 18:24. Read these verses and underline words or phrases that describe how an accountability group can work.

As iron sharpens iron,
so one man sharpens another (Proverbs 27:17).

Plans fail for lack of counsel,
but with many advisers they succeed (Proverbs 15:22).

Wounds from a friend can be trusted,
but an enemy multiplies kisses (Proverbs 27:6).

A man of many companions may come to ruin,
but there is a friend who sticks closer than a brother
(Proverbs 18:24).

What size should an accountability group be? If it's too large, people cannot share personally and deeply. If it's only two men, they can easily lead one another astray. As a friendship between two men grows, they tend to overlook each other's faults. So, there's strength in numbers. I suggest four-man accountability groups that meet weekly or at least biweekly.

To whom are you accountable as I've described accountability? List three or four men who know you well and with whom you're compatible.

_____

_____

Would you be willing to take the risk and start an accountability group? For additional help call our office at 1-800-9-AWAKEN and request a complimentary copy of our equipping newsletter entitled, *How to Start an Accountability Group*. Commit to God to seek the counsel and encouragement of other Christian men and to become a counselor and encourager in return.

The Bottom Line
- Some issues in life can't be handled by self-examination and the study of God alone.
- Sometimes we need a friend to help us see things more clearly.
- There is power in vulnerability, strength in numbers, and safety in visibility.
- Accountability means to be regularly answerable for each of the key areas in your life to qualified people.

THE DISCIPLINE OF BIBLE STUDY

Many men never understand what the Bible says. They have respect for the Bible but no knowledge of its contents. The Bible presents a detailed picture of who we are, who God is, and how we should live in response. In biblical history, when the people of God did not study the Word of God, they always went in search of many schemes. Every man did what seemed right in his own eyes. Men called evil good, and good evil. The Bible says a man is the slave of whatever has mastered him (1 Peter 2:19). Better to be mastered by the Bible.

Most men do not have the time, interest, or aptitude to dig out the meat of a passage. Private study is important but can lead to error. It is also easy to lapse if you try to study only on your own.

◆

**A group Bible study provides balance and insight that
you can't get on your own.**

A good community or church men's or couples' Bible study is a tremendous way to:
- learn God's truth through Bible study.
- be discipled by a more experienced person.
- have role models to observe and emulate.
- have counselors to bounce ideas off of.
- group with other men or couples for fellowship.
- carry one another's burdens.
- be accountable by asking one another the right questions.
- have a sounding board for understanding biblical concepts.

Briefly list the characteristics of a good experience you have had in a Bible study group or class.

_____

_____

What keeps you (and your wife) from being in a Bible study setting? Check those things that hinder you most often.

❑ Too busy   ❑ Not aware of a good study to be in
❑ Not interested   ❑ Afraid of getting too close to others
❑ Don't want others to see my lack of biblical knowledge
❑ Don't want to be judged or criticized

Resolve to eliminate these hurdles and get involved in a Bible study.

What do Christians do when they come together for study and worship? Read 1 Corinthians 14:26 and list the things Christians do when they come together.

Let the word of Christ dwell in you   _____
richly as you teach and admonish one   _____
another with all wisdom, and as you   _____
sing psalms, hymns, and spiritual songs _____
with gratitude in you hearts toward   _____
God (1 Corinthians 14:26).   _____

In studying the Bible together, some groups have one teacher and others share the teaching responsibilities. No teacher can do all the work for you. Let me suggest tools to help you study on your own and prepare for group study. Instead of just listing these tools, see if you can figure out what each resource does. Try to put the appropriate letters by the resources described at the top of the next page (an answer key is located at the bottom of the next page).

a. Bible Dictionary
b. Concordance
c. Bible Atlas
d. Commentary
e. Introduction to the New Testament
f. Topical Bible
g. Gospel Parallels
h. Introduction to the Old Testament
i. Study Bible

____ 1. Introduction to each book of the Bible and verse by verse comments on the meaning and history behind the text.

____ 2. Each of the synoptic Gospels (Matthew, Mark, Luke) is printed side by side to compare similarities and differences.

____ 3. Major passages related to a Bible theme or doctrine are listed and printed out.

____ 4. Definitions of word, terms, and places in the Bible.

____ 5. Ancient cultures; their relationship to Old Testament history.

____ 6. History behind the New Testament, including travels of Paul, the synoptic problem, the history of the early church.

____ 7. Maps detailing the Exodus or the travels of Paul, for example.

____ 8. Listing of all the passages that have a particular word in them, e.g. *apostle*.

____ 9. A Bible with extensive notes, articles, and reference material for study.

Most of these resources can be obtained in paperback from your local Christian book store. Talk with your pastor, group leader, or class teacher for recommendations on good reference material and a translation of the Bible they recommend. Some excellent Bible study software is available if you have a computer.

If you are not already in a Bible study, give prayerful consideration to this community spiritual discipline of personal growth.

Bible studies and accountability groups have the same end in mind—to make men into spiritual leaders and disciples—but they approach discipleship from very different angles. It takes time to study the Bible. It takes time to hold one another accountable. Personally, I think it would be quite difficult to accomplish both at the same time. The risk is to not do either in enough depth to really changes lives.

(Answers: 1. d.; 2. g.; 3. f.; 4. a.; 5. h.; 6. e.; 7. c.; 8. b.; 9. i.)

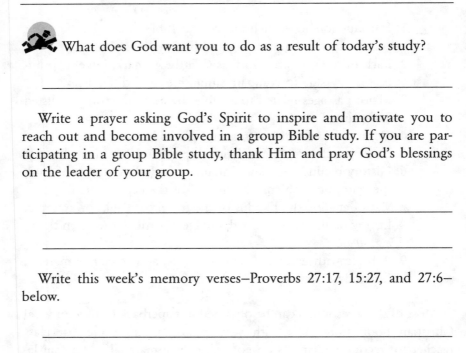

What does God want you to do as a result of today's study?

_____

_____

Write a prayer asking God's Spirit to inspire and motivate you to reach out and become involved in a group Bible study. If you are participating in a group Bible study, thank Him and pray God's blessings on the leader of your group.

_____

_____

Write this week's memory verses—Proverbs 27:17, 15:27, and 27:6—below.

_____

_____

_____

The Bottom Line
- Most men do not have the time, interest, or aptitude to dig out the meat of each passage.
- It is also easy to lapse if you try to study only on your own.
- A group Bible study provides balance and insight that you can't get on your own.
- It is difficult to accomplish true accountability and true in-depth group Bible study at the same time.

THE DISCIPLINE OF CHURCH: WORSHIP

A navy man once told me that fewer than five percent of the crew attends church when a vessel is in port. When out at sea, the number doubles to 10 percent. When a destroyer in their fleet was sunk, however, 100 percent of the crew attended services.

If we are not careful, we can end up using the Emergency Broadcasting System of Christianity. Unless we have a felt need, we often don't worship God. We err when we put the emphasis on us instead of God.

◆

**Whether we *feel* the need to worship God or not,
we *have* a need to do so.**

The Greek word for church, *ekklesia*, appears 95 times in the New Testament. *Church* means the body of believers, not the buildings where the believers assemble.

Have you considered the role your church plays in your life and the life of your family and friends? Here is a list of some ministries in most churches. Check the ones that have touched you and your family.

❑ Teaching the Bible
❑ Worshipping God
❑ Lord's Supper or Eucharist
❑ Reaching people for Christ
❑ Performing baptisms
❑ Utilization of spiritual gifts
❑ Marriage ceremonies
❑ Spiritual instruction in raising children
❑ Hospital, nursing home, crisis visitation, funeral services
❑ Meeting needs of those experiencing difficult times
❑ Counseling
❑ Equipping for ministry
❑ Discipleship
❑ Doctrine training

Write a prayer thanking God for all the ministries the church has provided for you and your family.

_____

_____

_____

The body of believers, *the ekklesia,* touches our lives significantly through worship, teaching, service, and fellowship. Before we can serve the Lord, we must worship Him. Jesus says, "Worship the Lord your God, and serve Him only" (Matthew 4:10). In worship, we bring God our sacrifices of praise and thanksgiving; our gifts of tithes and offerings; our time for intimacy and closeness with Him; and the opportunity to hear the proclamation of God's Word. Most of all, in worship we experience God's presence. We are never changed in the presence of men but we are changed in God's Presence.

Write your definition of worship. _____

_____

_____

Compare your definition to the following Scriptures about worship. Underline words in these passages that you used in your definition. Circle words you would like to include.

Every day they continued to meet together in the temple courts. They broke bread in their homes and ate together with glad and sincere hearts, praising God and enjoying the favor of all the people. And the Lord added to their number daily those who were saved (Acts 2:46-47).

God is spirit, and his worshippers must worship him in spirit and in truth (John 4:24).

Speak to one another with psalms, hymns, and spiritual songs. Sing and make music in your heart to the Lord, always giving thanks to God the Father for everything, in the name of our Lord Jesus Christ (Ephesians 5:19-20).

Hebrews 10:25 also warns, "Let us not give up meeting together as some are in the habit of doing."

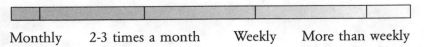 How faithful are you in public worship? Put an x on the bar where you are and a check where you need to be.

Monthly   2-3 times a month   Weekly   More than weekly

If other things take priority over corporate worship, we need to be reminded that one essential purpose of our lives is to worship God. We cannot find real fulfillment if we don't worship Him.

Take time to prepare for worship. Bring with you a desire to worship God and focus your heart on Him. Ask God in prayer to prepare your heart for worship.

Carefully read the following passage from Psalm 51. Then pray it as a closing prayer for today's study.

> O Lord, open my lips,
>   and my mouth will declare your praise.
> You do not delight in sacrifice, or I would bring it;
>   you do not take pleasure in burnt offerings.
> The sacrifices of God are a broken spirit;
>   a broken and contrite heart, O God, you will not despise
>   (Psalm 51:15-17).

Review today's study. What was the most meaningful statement or Scripture you read?

_____

_____

What does God want you to do as a result of today's study?

_____

_____

_____

The Bottom Line
- Unless we have a felt need, we often don't worship God.
- Whether we *feel* the need to worship God or not we *have* a need to do so.
- If other things take priority over corporate worship, we need to be reminded that one essential purpose of our lives is to worship God.

THE DISCIPLINE OF CHURCH: FELLOWSHIP

Do you think it is possible to be a "Lone Ranger" Christian? God called us in Jesus Christ into a community called the *ekklesia*, the church. We live in an age in which individualism is often valued more than community. Yet the Bible emphasizes corporate identity—we are one in Christ Jesus. Jesus tells us that when two or more are gathered in His Name He is in their midst (see Matthew 18:20). We are instructed to pray and worship together. Jesus sent out His disciples two-by-two to witness. We are not called individuals but a body in Christ. A church is a place to belong, to be a member of the body.

We live in an age when the individual is held in higher regard than the institution. Baby boomer and baby buster lack of loyalty to institutions in general has spilled over into the church. In fact, many churches don't even require formal membership. This is neither safe nor healthy.

It is regrettable that culture has had more influence upon the church than the church has had upon the culture in our generation. Although 94 percent of Americans say they believe in God, an amazing 80 percent of them expect to arrive at their religious beliefs independent from any church.[1] But where else would we find a more dependable guide for determining what we believe?

A great need today is that Christians revalue the church—recognize the importance of membership (including commitment, loyalty, and accountability) in a vital body of believers. Those who have worked around Christians who try to make it on their own without commitment to a local body of believers, as I have, are weary of being asked to pick up the broken pieces of lives shattered by lack of accountability.

Fellowship is more than a covered dish supper or men's pancake breakfast. Biblical fellowship, *koinonia*, is building deep, caring relationships with others in the community of the church. Let's look at three aspects of fellowship. First, **fellowship happens as we minister to one another using our spiritual gifts**. Some men feel they have nothing to give in a church except their money. That's incorrect. Believers are given wonderful gifts by the Holy Spirit to share in ministry with others. If you are unaware of your spiritual gifts or you need to know more about spiritual gifts, talk with a minister in your church. You might also check your local book store for material on discovering and applying your gifts.

Second, **fellowship allows us to be accountable to other believers under the authority of Jesus Christ.** Instead of going off doing our own thing, we are under the spiritual authority and guidance of Jesus Christ and the persons He has given to shepherd us. Jesus Christ is the head of the church: "And he is the head of the body, the church" (Colossians 1:18). Christ has given pastors, teachers, elders, and deacons to help us grow spiritually.

List those in spiritual authority over you and how they nurture your life and hold you accountable.

Name   **Nurtures me spiritually by:**

_____   _____

_____   _____

_____   _____

_____   _____

Finally, **fellowship gives us the opportunity to develop deep and life-long friendships in Jesus Christ.** We need Christian friends who can encourage and edify us. If you have a men's ministry in your church, support it (if not, should you start one?). The relationships you build when you don't necessarily need anything will be a blessing when you do.

Supporting a local church through membership—not merely attendance—represents the most significant of the public spiritual disciplines.

◆

If we truly love Christ, we will want to be around His people.

This week we have discussed significant reasons for belonging to a local church. If you do not belong, discuss these reasons with your wife and family. Prioritize what's important. Make a commitment to join a local church.

If you do belong to a church, check one area that needs more commitment and cultivation from you.

_____ Worship: Experiencing the presence of God

_____ Fellowship: Encouragement from God and from other believers

_____ Growth: Knowledge of God from His Word

_____ Service: Work for God

_____ Accountability: Persevere in God

Pray thanking God for the Body of Christ and how the church has ministered to you and your family over the years.

The Bottom Line
- Baby boomer and baby buster lack of loyalty to institutions in general has spilled over into the church.
- A great need today is that Christians revalue the church.
- The relationships you build when you don't necessarily need anything will be a blessing when you do.
- If we truly love Christ, we will want to be around His people.

¹Robert N. Bellah, et. al., *Habits of the Heart* (NY: Harper and Row, 1985), 228.

This week you discovered ...
- the importance of maintaining public spiritual disciplines.
- how to be accountable.
- how to incorporate group Bible study into your spiritual pilgrimage.
- the value of the church in your and your family's lives.
- the importance of worship and fellowship with other believers.

What does God want you to do in response to this week's study?

Recite Proverbs 27:17, 15:22, and 27:6 and meditate on these verses as your closing thought today.

DISCOVERING YOUR CALLING

A couple of years ago Dave recommitted his life to follow Christ—a "no regrets, no retreat" surrender to Jesus. Although he didn't actually hear any words, he sensed the Lord saying, *You believe in Me.*

Hungry to grow in the knowledge of God, Dave and his wife enrolled in a 34-week Bible study program offered by their church. He devoured everything thrown at him. He also continued to attend our TGIF Men's Bible Study. At the end of the 34 weeks, he sensed the Lord saying, again without words, *You know Me.*

In the process of growing in the Lord, Dave sensed a deeply felt desire—almost a drive—to not only know God, but to do something for Him as an expression of gratitude. Eventually, he felt consumed by the desire to serve the Lord. He began exploring personal ministry options, yet none of them worked out. Week after week went by. Weeks turned into months. He began to get discouraged. He began to wonder if it was all a bunch of emotion on his part. He began to doubt. Second thoughts crept into his mind.

One day Dave was earnestly praying about not finding an avenue to serve Christ. As he poured out his heart, hurt, desire, and doubt to the Lord, Dave again sensed the Lord speaking to him, *You don't trust me.*

Wow! thought Dave. *God is right! I have stopped trusting Him to show me what He would have me do in His good timing. Instead, I have taken charge of my life again.* Another lesson learned.

By divine "coincidence" the lesson at the next Friday morning Bible study centered on providing for our families by discipling them—to make our families a personal ministry (see 1 Timothy 5:8). Dave felt as if someone had hit him with a hammer. It finally sank in what the Lord wanted him to do. He realized that before he tried to save the world, he had better devote some time to his own family.

Curiously, shortly after Dave made this adjustment, the Lord began to shape a new idea in his mind about reaching his peers at work.

Lately, Dave spends a lot of time networking with other Christians in his career field, talking over the best ways to have an evangelistic witness, especially at trade shows. He also has begun to see intrinsic value in the work he does—that it is part of his calling.

The exact strategy has not yet surfaced, but Dave thinks God has clearly given him a vision for serving Christ, both in his family and in his occupation.

What is your calling? How does God desire that you serve Him in your family, your work, and through ministry opportunities?

As you study this week, you will:
• Understand the various aspects of your calling in Jesus Christ;
• Explore what the Bible says about calling;
• Look at your career as a calling;
• Discover what building the kingdom and tending the culture have to do with calling;
• Uncover your call to service and look at 12 suggestions to discover your calling.

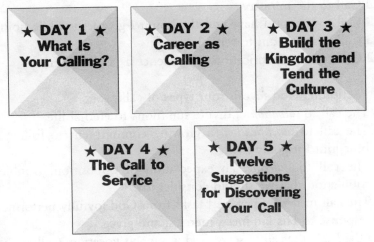

★ DAY 1 ★
What Is
Your Calling?

★ DAY 2 ★
Career as
Calling

★ DAY 3 ★
Build the
Kingdom and
Tend the
Culture

★ DAY 4 ★
The Call to
Service

★ DAY 5 ★
Twelve
Suggestions
for Discovering
Your Call

Memorize, meditate, and focus your attention on this passage:
    You did not choose me, but I chose you and appointed you
    to go and bear fruit—fruit that will last (John 15:16).

WHAT IS YOUR CALLING?

There is a myth that states, "As long as we do it honestly, everyone is free to pursue his own self-interests." Sometimes this is called *principled self-interest*. Actually, this is a form of capitalism, but it is not Christianity.

The Christian is not free to pursue his self-interests. The Christian has been bought with a price. He belongs to the King. He is called to deny himself, take up his cross, and follow Jesus. God has a plan for your life.

◆

God's calling includes all of life: your vocation, your family, your church, your community, your country, and your ministry.

When you hear the term *calling*, what comes to mind? Check which of the following you think of most often.
- ❏ Call to follow Jesus
- ❏ Call to the ministry
- ❏ Call to the job I have and the honor I give Jesus while doing it
- ❏ Call to how I am to serve Jesus
- ❏ Call to the sanctification I experience as a Christian

In Scripture, God reveals four types of calling:
- The call to *salvation:* a divine summons to eternal life.
- The call to *sanctification:* a growing commitment to follow God's blueprint for godly living.
- The call to *suffering:* an expectation of opposition, trouble, and tribulation that we should consider joy.
- The call to *service:* personal tasks from God joyfully performed as a response to His kindness, mercies, and grace.

In the Bible the call to serve God is a man's vocation. Calling includes all the tasks we do, not only in ministry but also in our work. In fact, for men of the Bible their work was a crucial part of their calling. Abraham served the Lord as a rancher. David served the Lord as a shepherd and king. Daniel served the Lord as a statesman. Jeremiah served the Lord as a prophet. Paul served the Lord as a tent-maker and evangelist. Peter served the Lord as a small businessman and disciple-maker. Their work and their service were one and the same.

It would be good to rediscover that the work we do is as much a part of our calling as is personal ministry. Below is a list of questions men frequently ask once that fire to serve the Lord starts to burn their hearts. Check those that most interest you.

❏ I want to serve the Lord, but what can I do?
❏ Wouldn't I have to be a minister to serve the Lord?
❏ I have the desire to serve God, but how do I go about it?
❏ What kind of personal ministry can I do?
❏ Is my work part of my calling?
❏ Why is it taking so long to get in gear?
❏ What is God's will for my life?
❏ What does the Bible say about all this?

Let's explore what the Bible has to say about man's call to serve. Listed below are some biblical principles about service and passages that illustrate these principles. Get your Bible and look up each passage. Match a Scripture with each principle by placing a letter in each blank. A passage may be used more than once.

Principle	Passage
_____ 1. God made us to serve Him.	a. 1 Corinthians 4:2
_____ 2. God has already determined what He wants us to do.	b. 2 Timothy 3:16-17
	c. 1 Peter 4:11
_____ 3. God wants each of us to bear fruit.	d. Romans 12:6
_____ 4. Some are called to speak, some to serve, and some to do both.	e. John 15:8
	f. Ephesians 2:10
_____ 5. The ultimate purpose of our service is to bring glory to God.	g. Romans 12:4-5
	h. 1 Peter 4:10
_____ 6. The earthly purpose of our calling is faithfully to serve others.	
_____ 7. God calls us to be faithful, not successful.	
_____ 8. God gives us different spiritual gifts.	
_____ 9. We serve God as part of a larger body.	
_____ 10. The Bible equips us to do good works.	

(Answers: 1. f.; 2. f.; 3. e.; 4. c.; 5. c.; 6. h.; 7. a.; 8. d.; 9. g.; 10. b.)

Look over these statements that describe God's purpose in calling us. Which one has the most impact on your life right now? Circle it. Which one is most difficult for you to live out? Underline it.

Sometimes it is difficult for us to imagine that God has such a profound purpose for our lives. It is impossible to fulfill His calling through our own plans and strength. We need God's strength and power to be the men He calls us to be. You may feel both awed and overwhelmed by what you read today. Or, you may be discouraged, wondering why you don't have a greater sense of purpose in your life. Regardless of your feelings, the greater truth is this: God gave His Son Jesus Christ so that His purposes for you might be fulfilled.

Review today's study. What was the most meaningful statement or Scripture you read?

_____

Say this verse as both a prayer and an affirmation.

"Being confident of this, that he who began a good work in [me] will carry it on to completion until the day of Christ Jesus" (Philippians 1:6).

The Bottom Line
- God's calling includes all of life: your vocation, your family, your church, your community, your country, and your ministry.
- God gives us personal tasks to perform joyfully as a response to His kindness, mercies and grace.
- It would be good to rediscover that the work we do is as much a part of our calling as is personal ministry.
- We need God's strength and power to be the men He calls us to be.

CAREER AS CALLING

When I stepped away from day-to-day business to devote myself full-time to helping men think more deeply about their lives, I thought I would wake up the next day feeling more spiritual—somehow holier. It never happened.

Then I supposed that when I looked into the mirror, I would see the faint outline of a halo. Oh, I didn't think anyone else would ever see it, but I thought for sure that I would. It never happened.

I thought my walk with Christ would soar to new heights since I was working directly for Him all day. It never happened.

I dreamed about how, once in ministry, I would never again have to go through that one day a week when I wanted to chuck the whole thing. It's true. I don't want to chuck the whole thing one day a week. Now I want to chuck it two days a week!

Actually, I feel no more called to writing, teaching, and speaking than I did to making investments in land and buildings. I am no more passionate about what I do now than about what I did before.

The Bible makes no distinction between sacred and secular. In the mind of God there is no such thing as a "secular" job. (Look up every reference to *secular* in a concordance—you won't find any.) Every vocation is holy to the Lord.

◆

**Every career should be seen first and foremost as
an avenue to bring glory to God.**

Many men who sense the desire to serve God welling up within them assume they must now do something else. This is rarely the case. For 99 percent of us, God probably wants us right where we are. Paul told the Corinthians: "Each one should retain the place in life that the Lord assigned to him and to which God has called him" (see 1 Corinthians 7:17, 20-21). Generally, a man should keep doing what he already does, but differently—with a whole new orientation to pleasing Christ.

Your occupation is part of your call to service. God intends you to be a witness for Jesus Christ and to minister wherever you work at whatever you do. You can minister effectively in your career. In fact, your vocation is a vital part of your ministry.

Check the ways in the following list that you have been able to reflect Christ-like character in your work.
❑ Share Jesus Christ with another person at work
❑ Be an example of Christian love and forgiveness
❑ Guard my tongue and not gossip
❑ Provide quality products and services to customers
❑ Be an example of integrity and honesty
❑ Increase profits and value for owners or shareholders
❑ Be a good steward of my company's funds
❑ Help grow the company to provide quality jobs for others

On the job your faith should season every action and word so that God will receive praise, glory, and honor. You don't have to force the word "Jesus" into every conversation, but His presence should be conspicuous to anyone giving it a moment's thought.

Scripture teaches that we should do everything as unto the Lord. The most menial task at work is done for His glory and praise. Describe something you dislike doing at work.

_____

_____

Describe how you might do that task to the glory of God.

_____

_____

Who is your boss? Do you work for yourself, or are you employed by someone else? Whether you are self-employed or work for a large or small company, chances are you are striving 'to be your own boss.' It seems that everybody wants to be independent and call their own shots.

Read the following Scripture and underline words that describe the "chain of command" for your work.

"Slaves, obey your earthly masters in everything; and do it, not only when their eye is on you and to win their favor, but with sincerity of heart and reverence for the Lord. Whatever you do, work at it with all your heart, as working for the Lord, not for men, since you know that you will receive an inheritance from the Lord as a reward" (Colossians 3:22-24).

Everyone is accountable to others in their work. Beyond this, we are accountable to God. It is the Lord we are serving. We are to serve our earthly boss because he holds God's proxy as our employer. But God still owns the company—He owns everything. He has the final interest in all things.

What is one step you need to take in the coming days that will give more glory and honor to the Lord in your career and work?

_____

Pray asking God to give you the strength and courage to take that step.

The Bottom Line
- In the mind of God there is no such thing as a "secular" job.
- Every career should be seen first and foremost as an avenue to bring glory to God.
- Many men who sense the desire to serve God welling up within them assume they must now do something else.
- Generally, a man should keep doing what he already does, but differently—with a whole new orientation to pleasing Christ.

BUILD THE KINGDOM AND TEND THE CULTURE

Lyle, who owns his own business, went through a spiritual renewal. He said, "The Lord has shown me that my business is my ministry. I am leading a Bible study at the office for anyone who wants to attend. And I have made it my goal to expose every vendor, employee, and key man to Jesus Christ." He also is having a leavening influence on his community by producing excellent work. He has become salt and light.

Jesus put the Great Commission like this: "Go and make disciples of all nations, baptizing them in the name of the Father and of the Son and of the Holy Spirit, and teaching them to obey everything I have commanded you" (Matthew 28:19-20). *God calls us to build His Kingdom— the Great Commission.*

Make a list of the things you do at work out of the overflow of your relationship with Jesus Christ.

_____

_____

In addition to the Great Commission, the Cultural Commission says we must manage the world as God's stewards. We find this commission in Genesis 1:28: "God blessed them and said to them, 'Be fruitful and increase in number; fill the earth and subdue it. Rule over the fish of the sea and the birds of the air and over every living creature that moves on the ground.'" *God calls us to tend the culture—the Cultural Commission.*

◆

God calls us to build the kingdom and tend the culture.

The two great themes of the Bible are *creation* and *redemption*. In recent generations we have put the emphasis on redemptive tasks—building the kingdom, winning people to faith, and fulfilling the Great Commission. (Whatever corrections we need to make, let's not stop doing these!)

However, we have neglected our creation tasks—tending the culture, preserving society, fulfilling the Cultural Commission (or Mandate). Perhaps the reason we have not invested in these things is that we don't tend to see any redemptive value in creation tasks like commerce, the trades, law, medicine, government, and the arts. This view makes a distinction between sacred and secular where God does not. Besides, look at the slough of problems we have in culture. Where is the leavening influence of Christian men?

Below is a list of cultural enterprises that Christian men could influence. Put a x on the bar to indicate how much Christian influence is at work in each arena at the present time.

Music

Significant Christian influence   Some Christian influence   No Christian influence

Art

Significant Christian influence   Some Christian influence   No Christian influence

Television

Significant Christian influence   Some Christian influence   No Christian influence

Movies

Significant Christian influence   Some Christian influence   No Christian influence

Medicine

Significant Christian influence   Some Christian influence   No Christian influence

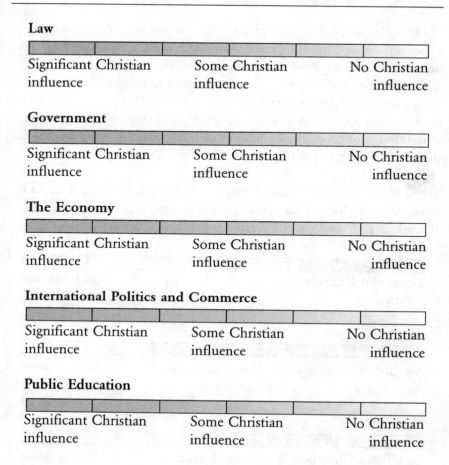

Law

| Significant Christian influence | Some Christian influence | No Christian influence |

Government

| Significant Christian influence | Some Christian influence | No Christian influence |

The Economy

| Significant Christian influence | Some Christian influence | No Christian influence |

International Politics and Commerce

| Significant Christian influence | Some Christian influence | No Christian influence |

Public Education

| Significant Christian influence | Some Christian influence | No Christian influence |

All the preceding creation tasks are very important to God and deserve Christian involvement and influence. Obviously, we cannot be involved in everything, but there are areas where we can be salt and light in the world. Let's be realistic. We spend most of our time at what have been erroneously called secular jobs. Most of our time on a day-to-day basis is spent in work that tends the culture rather than in work that wins the lost. These jobs are creation tasks, not redemption tasks—though we may end up sharing our faith with coworkers. More of us need to recognize that our work is our calling, and to serve as though serving Christ, not men (see Colossians 3:23).

One biblical principle that applies to all of life's activities, whether involved in the Great Commission or the Cultural Commission, is

1 Corinthians 10:31, "So whether you eat or drink or whatever you do, do it all for the glory of God."

To devalue creation tasks is to say our work doesn't matter to God. That's simply not true. Since Adam began tending the garden, man's work has been a holy calling.

Actually, God never calls any man to either redemptive tasks or creation tasks. Rather, God calls us to both build the kingdom and tend the culture. Further, we often get this backward—we tend to build the culture and tend the kingdom. This won't do. We need an aggressive approach to both the evangelistic gospel and the social gospel

The Underground Railroad helped 40,000 slaves escape to Canada. A young white man named Ross took a special interest in a slave named Thomas. Thomas asked him, "Why are you doing this, Mr. Ross?"

"Ever since I was a boy I wanted to be in this cause," he answered. "But now that I'm involved, it's more than a cause. It's about people."

Remember why you do what you do. All callings, done well, will point men to Christ.

List some of the major tasks you do at work.

_____

_____

_____

For each task, briefly describe what it would mean to do your work to the glory of God. How could this task be a testimony to others about the influence of Christ in your life?

Review today's study. What was the most meaningful statement you read?

_____

_____

Reword the statement into a prayer response to God.

_____

_____

What does God want you to do as a result of today's study?

_____

_____

The Bottom Line
- God calls us to build the kingdom and tend the culture.
- The two great themes of the Bible are creation and redemption.
- More of us need to recognize that our work is our calling, to serve as though serving Christ, not men.

THE CALL TO SERVICE

When God calls, He rarely sends right away. Instead, we go through a season of equipping in which we encounter delays, uncertainties, and hardships. Sometimes this equipping period lasts a long time.

◆

The call to service develops in three phases: calling, equipping, and sending.

Consider a time in your life when God called you to serve Him in a specific area of ministry. Briefly write the process you went through when God called, equipped, and sent you.

_____

_____

I know this idea of waiting is not one that we find appealing, but usually the bigger the calling, the longer the equipping. Why is that? We can learn from Moses, Abraham, and Joseph.

Delays and Waiting
God gave a young, virile Moses the vision that he would be the deliverer of his people held as slaves in Egypt. Moses lived in Pharaoh's household but remained true to his faith. One day he killed an Egyptian he found beating a fellow Jew. Surely that was the beginning of the vision to serve God. But there was too much "Moses" in Moses. So God sent him into the Midian wilderness for 40 years for a time of equipping—a time of working some things into and out of Moses' life.

When God was ready to send Moses, we find a much humbler man. In fact, the Bible says Moses was the most humble man who ever lived. That's what 40 years in the wilderness will do for you.

Equipping takes so long because sending demands so much. When God sends, He faithfully builds into a person's life all that is needed to go. This takes time. Never ask God to send you before you're ready to go.

The Bible says much about waiting. Read the following Scriptures and write down what they say about waiting.

> Be still before the Lord and wait patiently for him; do not fret when men succeed in their ways, when they carry out their wicked schemes (Psalm 37:7).

> But as for me, I watch in hope for the Lord, I wait for God my Savior; my God will hear me (Micah 7:7).

> Keep yourselves in God's love as you wait for the mercy of our Lord Jesus Christ to bring you to eternal life (Jude 1:21).

_____

_____

Uncertainties

God called Abraham to leave his native country and "go to the land I will show you" (Genesis 12:1). In other words, Abraham began his journey not knowing the destination. He was going, not knowing.

Like Abraham, we don't fully know where God is sending us. If we have it all planned out, it is likely in the flesh.

God gave Abraham a vision for becoming the father of a great nation. He remained childless in his old age, but the Bible says he kept believing God. Eventually, his wife gave birth to a boy, Isaac, who had a son, Jacob, who was later renamed Israel, whose offspring did become a great nation.

If God has put a vision to serve Him in your heart, however dim or foggy, keep the faith and never give up. The vision from God rarely comes clearly. He initially gives us enough vision to begin but not to see the end. If He gave us the whole vision at once, we would depend upon ourselves instead of Him. Also, it might scare the wits out of us!

Think of a time when God gave you an idea or a dream, but you had to act on faith and not by sight. Only later did you see and understand God's plan in all that happened. Briefly describe that experience.

_____

_____

Hardships

Though we can find enormous personal satisfaction, the ultimate purpose of our service is not for our benefit, but for God's. Because of this, our service often is filled with hardships. We see an example of this in Joseph.

God gave a young, boastful Joseph a vision of ruling over his family. That must have been the last thing on his mind when his brothers sold him as a slave to a passing caravan. That must have been the last thing on his mind when his owner Potiphar's wife accused him of rape and he went to prison. God was working some things into Joseph's life, and some things out of Joseph's life.

Then God sent Joseph. Miraculously, he rose to become second only to Pharaoh in the kingdom of Egypt. When his brothers finally showed up in Egypt looking for food because of a famine in their own land, Joseph could say of their sin against him, "You meant it for harm, but God meant it for good—for the saving of many lives."

Hardships, suffering, trials, and tests refine our faith and character for serving God. Read Romans 5:3-5 below. Summarize how hardships produce character and prepare us for God's calling on our lives.

"Not only so, but we also rejoice in our sufferings, because we know that suffering produces perseverance; perseverance, character; and character, hope. And hope does not disappoint us, because God has poured out his love into our hearts by the Holy Spirit, whom he has given us" (Romans 5:3-5).

_____

_____

We must go through hardship because the people God calls us to minister to go through hardships. Through hardship, God strengthens our character so we can comfort others with the comfort we have received (see 2 Corinthians 1:3-4).

Write a prayer thanking God for the hardships, uncertainties, and delays which have helped shape your character and experience for His calling in your life.

_____

_____

Review today's study. What was the most meaningful Scripture you read?

_____

_____

Write this week's memory verse—John 15:16—below and meditate on its meaning for your life.

_____

_____

The Bottom Line
- The call to service develops in three phases: calling, equipping, and sending.
- When God calls, He rarely sends right away.
- Never ask God to send you before you're ready to go.
- If God has put a vision to serve Him in your heart, however dim or foggy, keep the faith and never give up.

TWELVE SUGGESTIONS FOR DISCOVERING YOUR CALL

Let's make some assumptions. Let's assume you know Christ, and you have a growing burden to serve Him. A man filled to the overflow will want to give it away. Let's assume you are not currently involved in a personal ministry. Let's also assume you are currently looking or are ready to look at your work as a sacred, holy calling. What would be the best way to discern how you can begin to produce fruit?

1. Employ the means of guidance. Here is a list of ways you may seek guidance from the Lord. Check those you currently use or plan to use.

❑ Scripture   ❑ The counsel of other Christians

❑ The Holy Spirit   ❑ Prayer

❑ Fasting   ❑ Discerning the doors God is opening

❑ Other:_____

Keeping the question before you, *God, what is Your calling for my life?*

2. Discover your spiritual gifts. God gives spiritual gifts, or special spiritual abilities, to every Christian. Make an effort to learn your spiritual gifts. Use them in your church, at work, and in your family.

If you already know your spiritual gifts, list them. _____

_____

Describe how you are using them to minister to others.

_____

_____

If you don't know your spiritual gifts, find out if your church offers training to help you. Ask your pastor, or check your local Christian book store for resources. Knowing your gifts will help you in your work as well as personal ministry.

3. Identify your motivated interests. Philippians 2:13 says, "It is God who works in you to will and to act according to his good purpose." In other words, God puts desires into our hearts to do His work. Pay attention to your desires. Pray over them and see if your motives are pure. Getting in touch with your motivated interests can help you direct career choices as well as choose personal ministry opportunities.

4. Complete your written life-purpose statement. To understand God's larger purpose for your life is to know why you are here and what your life is about. Think of a key verse that motivates your purpose in life. Formulate a sentence describing God's purpose for your life.

Key life verse: _____

God's purpose for my life: _____

5. Keep a journal. Consider keeping a written journal of Scriptures that touch you, ways God moves in your life, and prayer requests with answers. Look for patterns or directions in which God is leading.

6. Keep driving toward the vision. Vision is a mental picture of a desirable future. Eventually, God will give you a picture of what He wants you to do. While the vision may not be completely clear at first, keep driving toward the vision, even if you must proceed slowly because you are in a fog.

◆

**Act in light of what you do know, rather than
not acting in light of what you don't know.**

A vision begins to fill in the specifics of how God wants you to implement His purpose for your life.

Briefly describe the vision God has given you.

God's vision for me is_____

7. Pray about what to do when strategy is unclear. When our vision is unclear, we must pray and wait. God is equipping us—preparing us—with all we will need to successfully fulfill the vision. God may keep things unclear for 40 years, as in the case of Moses. Keep moving with what you've seen so far, while praying for what you still need to see.

8. Reorganize work life to allow for personal ministry. Don't be so bogged down in work you never have time to serve in ministry capacities beyond your work. Mark on the bar with an x where you are right now.

My work keeps me   I have time in my schedule
from personal ministry.   for personal ministry.

If you can, consider making a professional "tithe" of your work time to specific ministry.

9. Employ the power of faith. After winning the U.S. Open and Wimbledon, top tennis pro Pete Sampras was asked if he thought he could win the Grand Slam (the four major championships) like his hero Rod Laver did in 1968. No one since Laver has won it.

Sampras answered no. That pretty well sealed his fate. The negative power of disbelief will cripple your vision. But the power of belief or faith is enormous. Faith is trusting that what God puts in your heart is within His power to bring about.

10. Maintain priorities. Regardless of the specific ministry or occupation God gives us, we all have inescapable priorities that we must not neglect: wives, children, our walk with Christ, personal finances, rest, exercise, and work. We must take responsibility for our own private lives and ordering our private worlds.

11. Expect opposition. Live your life in light of the vision God has given you. Don't let opposition deter you. Remember Nehemiah's rebuilding the walls around Jerusalem? He said, "We prayed to our God and posted a guard day and night to meet this threat" (Nehemiah 4:9). The enemy was there, but Nehemiah was prepared and continued with God's vision for him.

Are you facing opposition right now? Who or what is it? _____

Have you let this opposition deter you from God's vision? _____

How can you get back on track? _____

12. Be willing to take some risks. After an invigorating discussion on calling, equipping, and sending, a man said with tears in his eyes, "But I'm just not feeling called."

The counsel to this man, who at the time was not serving the Lord at all, was, "Do something!"

Many men never attempt anything significant fearing they might fail. They would rather be perfect in potentiality than imperfect in actuality.

The Bottom Line

1. Employ the means of guidance.
2. Discover your spiritual gifts.
3. Identify your motivated interests.
4. Complete your written life-purpose statement.
5. Keep a journal.
6. Keep driving toward the vision.
7. Pray about what to do when strategy is unclear.
8. Reorganize work life to allow for personal ministry.
9. Employ the power of faith.
10. Maintain priorities.
11. Expect opposition.
12. Be willing to take some risks.

 This week you discovered ...
• the various aspects of your calling in Jesus Christ.
• your career as a calling.
• how to determine your call to service for Christ.
What does God want you to do as a result of this week's study?

REASSESSING MY SPIRITUAL LIFE

This study has been devoted to the Season of Rebuilding. As we explored this season of a man's life, we looked closely at our conversion to Jesus Christ; our relationship with God and others; our private and public disciplines; and our calling to personal ministry and to tending the culture.

Some tough and difficult questions have been faced and a time of spiritual growth has occurred. This final week of study will be a time of review and reassessment. You will have the opportunity to recall from your weekly study what you learned and how you applied that over the past five weeks in your personal walk with Jesus Christ.

Every Christian man goes through a season of rebuilding periodically in his spiritual life. Not every area will be addressed each time, but critical parts of our spiritual lives may be in disrepair and need rebuilding by the power of God's Spirit and our willingness to be convicted, corrected, and renewed by the Lord.

This week you will:

- Review what you have studied;
- Renew your commitment to grow and mature in your spiritual life;
- Pray through areas that need rebuilding spiritually;
- Commit to a personal ministry and call to serve through tending the culture;
- Move toward taking new steps of devotion to Jesus Christ.

★ DAY 1 ★
Four Crucial
Conversions

★ DAY 2 ★
Restoring
Relationships

★ DAY 3 ★
Three Private
Spiritual
Disciplines

★ DAY 4 ★
Three Public
Spiritual
Disciplines

★ DAY 5 ★
Discovering
Your Calling

Memorize, meditate on, and implement these verses this week.

> Search me, O God, and know my heart;
>   test me and know my anxious thoughts.
> See if there is any offensive way in me,
>   and lead me in the way everlasting (Psalm 139:23-24).

As you conclude the final week of this study, it's my prayer that the areas of your life that need spiritual growth and refreshment will be revealed and renewed. May Christ richly bless you as you grow through this season of rebuilding.

FOUR CRUCIAL CONVERSIONS

During Week 1 of this study, you explored four crucial "conversions" that need to take place in the Season of Rebuilding. Today, let's review the main ideas from that week.

◆

Day 1: The only thing worse than flesh is pious flesh.

Many times we are shaped more by the culture than by Christ. This is especially true in four crucial areas of life. We grow in Christ as our hearts, minds, calendars, and wallets are changed, converted, and made new.

Jesus calls men to a radically different way of thinking and living. This change is nothing to fear. In exchange for all the worldly fleshly desires, we will be filled with the fruit of the Spirit. We will increasingly become like Jesus, transformed into His image.

◆

Day 2: What Christ wants most is not what we can do for Him. He wants us.

Perhaps the greatest risk of walking with Jesus is that we would lose our first love. What starts out as a wonderful love relationship is reduced to an endless repetition of religious tasks and activities—all intended to please Him. It is not enough to just try to please Jesus. You must also give Him your heart.

On page 15 (week 1, day 2), you listed the qualities you expect from a best friend, and then used them to evaluate your relationship with Christ. How has your relationship with Christ changed during these last 5 weeks?

_____

_____

We serve God because we love Him. Out of our overflow of loving Jesus, His love compels us to do something wonderful for Him because of the rich deposits of gratitude building up in our hearts. Where are you in your love relationship with Jesus?

◆

Day 3: It is not enough to give Jesus your heart. You must also give Him your head.

Biblical Christianity is a thinking man's religion. It consists of specific, knowable truths. It is crucial to know what we believe and why. It is essential to the work of God's kingdom to think and decide rightly.

Critical to this is what you choose to put into your mind or what you allow your mind to dwell upon in your thought life. Read books that teach concepts from a Biblical worldview. Develop a quiet time each day to pray and study God's Word. Spend time in a Christian Bible study listening to God's Word being discussed. Do the things that will help you grow to be able to "take every thought captive" for Jesus Christ.

◆

Day 4: It is not enough to give Jesus your heart and your head. You must also give Him control over your time.

The way we invest our time says a lot about who's in charge of our lives. Many Christian men have yet to really settle this issue in their lives.

If Jesus stood in front of you, what might He say to you about the use of your time? Would Jesus confront you about wasting precious time?

How do you give your calendar to Jesus? If your heart and your mind have truly been converted, your calendar will follow. You convert your calendar by telling Jesus, "I will go anywhere You want me to go, do anything You want me to do, and be anything you want me to be." Have you done this?

◆

Day 5: God owns everything and calls us to be stewards of 100 percent of our money.

Our Christian culture tends to teach that we own our money and should give some of it back to God. This is not what the Bible teaches.

A steward is a manager. God allows us to manage and control some of His financial resources during our lives. It is our responsibility to manage these in a way that is in line with His purposes and goals for our lives. One way to evaluate if your heart has been truly converted is to answer the question, "Has your wallet been converted too?"

What will happen if we yield control of our money to Jesus? He will draw us closer to the safety of His pasture. He will release us from bondage to money. He will set us free to serve Him financially with gladness.

How have you grown in your understanding of what it means to become like Jesus? Briefly describe a change in your attitude or actions that illustrates what God is teaching you.

_____

_____

When we truly follow Christ, our hearts, minds, calendar, and wallets come with us. Consider these four crucial areas in your own life. Are you being pressured into the mold of our culture or are you growing into the image and likeness of Christ?

Throughout the study I have provided a summary of each day's material called "The Bottom Line." During these last five days, I want you to create your own "bottom line." What one truth has been most meaningful to you during each week of your study? At the end of each day this week, you will have an opportunity to write that truth. Reflect on what has been important to you. Ask God to help you live that truth each day.

The Bottom Line

_____

_____

RESTORING RELATIONSHIPS

Of all the areas that suffer from poor choices, the one that suffers most is our relationships. Even though we maintain a right relationship with God through recommitment, we are not automatically in right relationship with one another. The second most important thing to our relationship with God is that we maintain right relationships with others.

During Week 2 of this study, you explored how to restore broken relationships in your life. Let's review the big ideas from that week.

◆

Day 1: It is a supreme act of courage to restore your relationships by demonstrating the love of Jesus Christ.

If you have made poor choices in the past, you may be experiencing hurt, brokenness, and pain in your relationships with family members and others. The kind of love we need to restore broken relationships is agape, or moral love. Agape love demonstrates responsibility and commitment. It is unconditional love that seeks the best for the other person.

At the core of agape love is the willingness to forgive. If you are waiting for the other person in a broken relationship to come to you, you may have to wait forever.

◆

Day 2: The Bible says reconciliation should precede worship.

We cannot worship God acceptably if we are at odds with someone. If we have broken relationships, the Scriptures command us to go and be reconciled first–before we worship.

Biblical love requires you to love first, in spite of the other person's response. Even if he or she refuses to respond, you still have the responsibility to love, forgive, and initiate healing.

On page 31 and 36, you described relationships in your life that needed restoration. What steps have you taken to restore the wounded relationship? On the top of the next page, describe what has taken place.

_____

_____

◆

Day 3: Listening is the oil that lubricates the process of restoring relationships.

One way we show unconditional love is by giving another person the right to speak and then listening attentively to what he or she has to say. Rebuilding relationships requires this kind of active listening.

In order to be reconciled you must understand the other person's point of view. He may not be acting rationally, but there are reasons why he does what he does.

Remember the following pointers for listening attentively.

- Make frequent eye contact with the other person.
- Have a pleasant look on your face.
- When they pause in their talking, paraphrase what you hear them saying. For example, "What I hear you saying is …"
- If you pick up feelings they do not articulate, you might say, "I sense you are feeling …"
- Don't interrupt or defend yourself.
- Once they have finished saying all they wish to say, express your feelings in "I" messages and do not project blame or accusations on them. For example, "I feel" or "I think."

Have you grown in your ability to listen to others? Briefly describe a recent situation where listening enabled you to build a stronger relationship with another person.

_____

_____

◆

Day 4: When we truly repent, we not only say we are sorry, but our actions change as well.

"I'm sorry" and "I forgive you" are key words in healing any relationship. While being sorry is enough to begin healing, it is not enough to finish the job.

To bring down the walls between us, we must initiate healing, listen attentively, and give the other person an opportunity to express their grievances, anger, hurt, and pain. Then we must express genuine remorse.

The biblical word for this is *repentance* which means to change direction and turn the other way. Without a willingness to change, there is no evidence of true remorse or repentance.

True repentance leads to an opportunity for forgiveness. It is by forgiving and asking forgiveness that relationships are healed. Until someone says, "I'm truly sorry. Please forgive me," there is a stalemate. Until the offended party says, "I forgive you," healing can't take place.

◆

Day 5: A tender man will persevere when reconciliation is not immediate.

One of the prices of hurting each other is that sometimes the wounds don't heal overnight. We can control ourselves, but we have no control over the response of the other person. We can only continue to respond in the Spirit.

Obviously, if we can avoid conflict in the first place, our relationships will be far better off. But conflict is part of life, so knowing how to deal with conflict is a critical part of living together.

On page 44 and 45, you developed some guidelines to help you deal with conflict. Have you implemented these in your life? Briefly describe a circumstance during the last 5 weeks where these guidelines helped you to deal with conflict in an appropriate way.

_____

_____

Jesus told us His desire for our relationships: "A new command I give you: Love one another. As I have loved you, so you must love one another" (John 13:34). It takes a strong, tender man – solid in his relationship with God–to have the courage to restore broken relationships in his life.

Recall the memory verse for this week–Matthew 5:23-24. Write it below and underline the action we are to take before we can offer our gift to God.

_____

_____

_____

Close with a prayer that God would continue to make you into the kind of man that restores relationships instead of breaking them. Pray that your life and relationships would be characterized by love, joy, and peace.

The Bottom Line

_____

_____

THREE PRIVATE SPIRITUAL DISCIPLINES

Satan is a fisherman—and we are the fish. He lets us grab the bait, but he doesn't try to set the hook right away. Instead, he lets us run until we lull ourselves into a false confidence. Then, just when we are sure it's safe, he sets the hook, and it's too late. All that's left is to reel us in.

In week 3 of this study, we discussed three private spiritual disciplines that can help us avoid temptation and stay on track. Let's review the big ideas from that week.

◆

Day 1: A spiritual battle can only be won with spiritual weapons.

We won't win the spiritual battle if we identify it as a worldly war. The Bible says, "For our struggle is not against flesh and blood, but against the spiritual forces of evil in the heavenly realms" (Ephesians 6:12).

We also won't win the battle if we fight with the wrong weapons. If your dog had fleas, you wouldn't try to get rid of them with a shotgun. You wouldn't try to get chinch bugs out of your lawn by using dynamite.

Ephesians 6:13-18 describes the spiritual weapons we have as soldiers of Jesus Christ.

> Therefore put on the full armor of God, so that when the day of evil comes, you may be able to stand your ground and after you have done everything, to stand. Stand firm then, with the belt of truth buckled around your waist, with the breastplate of righteousness in place, and with your feet fitted with the readiness that comes from the gospel of peace. In addition to all this, take up the shield of faith, with which you can extinguish all the flaming arrows of the evil one. Take the helmet of salvation and the sword of the Spirit, which is the word of God. And pray in the Spirit on all occasions with all kinds of prayers and requests. With this in mind, be alert and always keep on praying for all the saints.

We also must know how to use these weapons effectively, and that involves discipline. Sometimes we must substitute discipline for a lack of natural interest. Spiritual discipline sometimes means: Do what you don't want to do, and you will become what you want to be. We practice discipline because we love Christ and desire to be more like Him.

◆

Day 2: The spiritual disciplines help us build a vital, moment-by-moment relationship with Christ.

In the same way that a farmer needs to put something back into the soil, so a believer needs to put something back into his relationship with God. The spiritual disciplines are the means by which we keep our relationship with the Lord fertile.

Spiritual disciplines are gifts, not requirements. They are means to a deeper fellowship with God, not ends in themselves. They do not save us, rather they provide us a way to pursue godliness in response to our salvation.

The Christian walk is a beautiful journey when we walk God's way. Walk it any other way, and it can be a desperate thing. Christ has given us great freedom. Freedom in Christ, though, is the liberty to do what we ought to do rather than what we want to do.

Three of the most important private spiritual disciplines are Bible study, prayer, and quiet time.

On page 55 you evaluated yourself in relation to these three disciplines. How would you rate yourself today? How have these disciplines made a difference in your life these last few weeks?

_____

_____

◆

Day 3: A man's life will never change in any significant way apart from the regular study of God's Word.

The Bible is the starting point of a life with God. The Bible communicates the truth of God to men in search of ultimate reality.

Frankly, after more than 20 years of following Christ, I find I no longer read my Bible. My Bible reads me. On its crinkly pages I see myself–my motives, my ambitions, my longings, my pain, my sufferings, my sins, my hope, my joy. As the rustling pages turn, I see God–His love, His forgiveness, His birth, His death, His resurrection, His sovereignty, His holiness, His character.

Through systematic study of the Bible, we develop a deep understanding of God and His ways. This knowledge of God becomes the foundation for our own walk of faith.

How regular has your Bible study become in recent weeks? Describe your Bible study routine.

◆

Day 4: Prayer should be the first thing we do, not the last.

Prayer changes us. Prayer breaks strongholds. Prayer determines the destinies of men, their families, their communities, and their nations. Though prayer is hard work, the benefits are well worth the cost.

If your prayer life is mechanical and unrewarding, consider these ideas. (1) Catchwords are a list of words, such as *praise, guidance, humility,* etc., that you write down in order to trigger things to pray over. (2) Writing down your prayers helps you see God working. (3) Praying Scripture helps you connect with the Lord as you repeat His Word back to Him in prayer. (4) Praying with a partner gives you accountability and encouragement to stick with it over the long-term.

How has your prayer life changed during this study? Which of these four ideas has been beneficial to you? Underline it. Briefly describe how it has brought renewed vitality to your prayer life.

◆

Day 5: A quiet time is a routine period of time set aside for meeting with God.

The quiet time is an accommodation to an overly busy culture. However, a regular time with the Lord can greatly enhance any man's walk with God. Each day we must resupply ourselves for the spiritual battle. To run out of spiritual food, ammunition, and strength can be catastrophic.

In Yosemite Park you can see grass growing out of the rocks up high. A tiny seed, by applying consistent pressure, works its roots into the rock and finds life. No matter how hard your circumstances, if you apply consistent pressure and have a daily quiet time, those roots will take hold for you.

On page 65, you wrote down a commitment concerning having a quiet time. How have you done in fulfilling your commitment? How has your quiet time made a difference in your life?

_____

_____

The Bottom Line

_____

_____

WHERE ARE MY PUBLIC DISCIPLINES GOING?

Ours is an anonymous, dangerous age. It is easy for us to get caught up in the daily grind of unthinking routine, and to live shallow and meaningless—even trivial—lives.

In week 4 of this study, you reflected on three public spiritual disciplines that can help a man stay focused on God's higher purposes for his life. Let's review the main ideas from that week.

◆

Day 1: A man who walks alone is like a lost sheep culled out from the safety of the flock by a wily wolf.

Women move about like sheep in the safety of groups, while men wander alone like proud lions through enemy territory. While we think we are like the lion, we are really like Mary's little lamb. To wander alone is neither wise nor safe.

The Bible repeatedly teaches that we have a responsibility to other Christians, and that they have a responsibility to us. We are to help each other grow in our relationship with Christ.

If you have bought into the idea that "faith is a private thing," the devil may be using this to make you vulnerable and to keep you apart from other men. A man can only be successful when he lives in community with other believers.

◆

Day 2: Accountability means to be regularly answerable for each of the key areas in your life to qualified people.

Some issues in life can't be handled by self-examination and the study of God alone. Sometimes we need a friend to help us see things more clearly.

The truth for the Biblical Christian is this: there is power in vulnerability, strength in numbers, and safety in visibility. The Bible puts it this way: "Plans fail for lack of counsel, but with many advisers they succeed" (Proverbs 15:22).

For accountability to work, men must be vulnerable, confidential, and confrontational. We must be willing to ask and answer the hard questions about what is really going on in our lives.

 On page 74, you listed men with whom you are or could be accountable. How has accountability benefited you these last few weeks?

◆

Day 3: A group Bible study provides balance and insight that you can't get on your own.

Most men do not have the time, interest, or aptitude to dig out the meat from a passage of Scripture. It is easy to lapse if you are only studying on your own, and private study can sometimes lead to error.

Bible study and accountability groups have the same end in mind—to make men into spiritual leaders and disciples. It takes time to study the Bible. A qualified Bible teacher invests himself in your life by doing the hard work necessary to teach the Word faithfully. Be sure to take advantage of Bible studies available in your church or community.

 Briefly describe a benefit from being in a group Bible study.

◆

Day 4: Whether we *feel* the need to worship God or not, we *have* a need to do so.

Many times we only stop to worship God when we have a need. We err when we put the emphasis on us instead of God.

In worship, we bring God our sacrifices of praise and thanksgiving; our gifts of tithes and offerings; our time for intimacy and closeness with Him; and our desire to hear the proclamation of God's Word. If other things are taking priority in your life over corporate worship, remember that one essential purpose of our lives is to worship God. We cannot find authentic fulfillment if we do not worship Him.

Briefly describe an especially meaningful worship time you have experienced in the last few weeks.

_____

_____

◆

Day 5: If we truly love Christ,
we will want to be around His people.

A great need today is for Christians to revalue the church–to recognize the importance of membership (including commitment, loyalty, and accountability). Those who have worked with Christians who try to make it on their own are weary of trying to pick up the broken pieces of lives shattered by a lack of accountability.

Biblical fellowship is building deep, caring relationships with other in the community of the church. We need Christian friends who can encourage and edify us. The relationships you build when you don't necessarily need anything will be a blessing when you do.

Supporting a local church through membership is the most significant of the public spiritual disciplines. Instead of going off and doing our own thing, we place ourselves under the authority and guidance of Jesus Christ and the persons He has given to shepherd us.

How are you doing in the area of public spiritual disciplines? Circle any of the three we have studied that still need work in your life.

Bible Study   Accountability   Church

The Bottom Line

_____

_____

DISCOVERING YOUR CALLING

God has a calling on your life. God desires that you serve Him through your family, work, and ministry opportunities.

In week 5 of our study, we examined some ideas about how to discover your calling. Let's review the main ideas of that week.

◆

Day 1: God's calling includes all of life: your vocation, your family, your church, your community, your country, and your ministry.

The Christian is not free to pursue his own self-interests. The Christian has been bought with a price. He is not his own. He belongs to the King. He is called to deny himself, take up His cross, and follow Jesus.

God calls us to serve Him. He gives us personal tasks to perform joyfully as a response to His kindness, mercies and grace.

Although it may sometimes be difficult for us to imagine that God has such a profound purpose for our lives, the greater truth is this: God gave His son Jesus Christ so that His purpose for you might be fulfilled. Paul expresses this same thought – "Being confident of this, that he who began a good work in you will carry it on to completion until the day of Christ Jesus" (Philippians 1:6).

◆

Day 2: Every career should be seen first and foremost as an avenue to bring glory to God.

Many men who sense the desire to serve God welling up within them assume they must now do something else. This is rarely the case. For 99 percent of us, God probably wants us to serve Him right where we are.

Your occupation is part of your call to service. Faith is not a private thing. On the job your faith should season every action and word so that God will receive praise, glory, and honor.

Everyone is accountable to others in their work. But beyond this, we are accountable to God. It is the Lord we are serving. We are to serve our earthly boss because he holds God's proxy as our employer. But God still owns the company—he owns everything. He has the final interest in all things.

Any job becomes exalted and meaningful if we realize that we are called to it by God. Evaluate your sense of God's calling on your career on the following continuum.

My job is drudgery.   I feel called to my job.

On page 92, you committed to a step that would give more glory and honor to the Lord in your career and work. Have you followed through with that step? What have been the results?

_____

_____

_____

◆

Day 3: God calls us to build the kingdom and tend the culture.

The two great themes of the Bible are creation and redemption. God calls us to creation tasks—preserving society, managing nature, tending the culture. He also calls us to redemptive tasks—building the kingdom, winning people to faith, fulfilling the Great Commission. We must be careful to balance these priorities in our lives.

Creation tasks are important to God and deserve Christian involvement and influence. Obviously, we cannot be involved in everything, but there are areas where we can be salt and light in the world. We spend most of our time at what have been erroneously called secular jobs. More of us need to recognize that our work is our calling, and to serve as though serving Christ, not men (see Colossians 3:23).

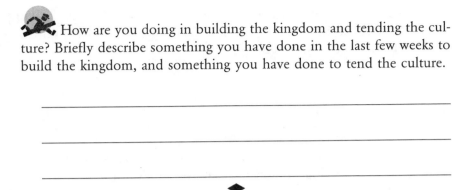 How are you doing in building the kingdom and tending the culture? Briefly describe something you have done in the last few weeks to build the kingdom, and something you have done to tend the culture.

_____

_____

_____

◆

Day 4: The call to service develops in three phases: calling, equipping, and sending.

When God calls, He rarely sends right away. Instead, we go through a season of equipping in which we encounter delays, uncertainties, and hardships. Sometimes this equipping period lasts a long time.

Equipping takes so long because sending demands so much. When God sends, He faithfully builds into a person's life all that's needed to go.

If God has put a vision to serve Him in your heart, however dim or foggy, keep the faith and never give up. The vision from God rarely comes clearly. He initially gives us enough vision to begin but not enough to see the end. If He gave us the whole vision at once, we would depend upon ourselves instead of Him. Also, it might scare the wits out of us!

We must go through hardship because the people God calls us to minister to go through hardships. Through hardship, God strengthens our character so we can comfort others with the comfort we have received.

Do you have a sense of God's calling on your life? Evaluate your calling by placing an x on the following bar to indicate where you are right now.

Being Called   Being Equipped   Being Sent

Are you satisfied with where God has you right now? Write a brief prayer to tell God how you feel about His calling on your life (afraid, doubtful, confused, joyous, confident, etc.).

_____

_____

◆

Day 5: Act in light of what you do know, rather than not acting in light of what you don't know.

In Day 5, I listed 12 suggestions to discovering your calling. They are:
Employ the means of guidance
Discover your spiritual gifts
Identify your motivating interests
Keep a journal
Complete your written life-purpose statement
Keep driving toward the vision
Pray about what to do when strategy is unclear
Reorganize work life to allow for personal ministry
Employ the power of faith
Maintain priorities
Expect opposition
Be willing to take some risks

Go back to page 106 and reflect on what you wrote in response to this study about God's calling. Do you have a greater sense of how God wants you to serve Him in a personal ministry? How are these 12 suggestions helping you to find God's calling on your life?

_____

_____

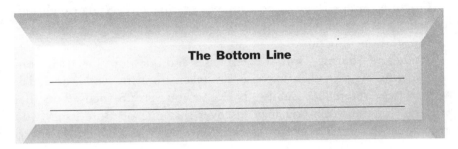 Review the Scripture verse for week 5 and underline the key words that describe how God calls us to service for Him.

"You did not choose me, but I chose you and appointed you to go and bear fruit—fruit that will last. Then the Father will give you whatever you ask in my name. This is my command: Love each other" (John 15:16-17).

The Bottom Line

_____

_____

What now? If you have not studied the other books in *The Seven Seasons of a Man's Life* collection, I encourage you to do so. The back cover of this book provides information to guide you in your selection.

As you turn now to that unique set of problems and opportunities that only you face, know that you are not alone, for God makes the seasons.

LEADER GUIDE

In the next six weeks, you will be exploring *The Season of Rebuilding* with a group of men. This leader guide is appropriate for home groups, men's Bible study groups, accountability groups, discipleship and prayer groups, and one-to-one discipling.

The Introductory Session is 90 minutes; weekly sessions are 50 minutes. Consider these suggestions for each session.

Opening Time–This can be a time of sharing and getting caught up on what's happened during the week. Each session has a suggested exercise for this opening time.

Study and Sharing Time–Key exercises and questions for discussion and sharing are provided. Exercises are taken from the weekly material with a page reference usually given. As your group focuses on the material for the week, you may discover that one or more issues will require more time. Do not be discouraged if the group does not cover all the material. The important thing is to discuss what the men in your group *need* to discuss.

Prayer and Closing Time–This is a time for men to pray together corporately or in pairs and to consider "next steps" in their spiritual walks with the Lord.

Each session needs a facilitator; it may be the same person or a different person for each session.

Before each group session the facilitator should:
• Pray for each group member.
• Complete all daily studies for that week.
• Encourage members to complete their work.
• Make handouts of the session material for those who want a separate copy, who forget their book, or who are new to the group.
• Contact members who were absent the last session.

Before the *first* group session, the facilitator should complete Week 1 of the material so he can speak from experience on how he set aside time daily to study.